Rivers Of Praise
Worship Through Movement

A Guide for Establishing a Lifestyle of Worship

Rachel L. Moore
Foreword by Steve Sawyer

Rivers Of Praise
Worship Through Movement

A Guide for Establishing a Lifestyle of Worship

Make His Praise Glorious!

Rachel. M.

Rivers Of Praise
Worship Through Movement

A Guide for Establishing a Lifestyle of Worship

Rachel L. Moore
Foreword by Pastor Steve Sawyer

 Dawn Treader Publications
He who treads the dawn is the Bright and Shining Morning Star™

A Ministry of Morning Star And Company, Inc.
Detroit   †   Pittsburgh   †   Cleveland

RIVERS OF PRAISE WORSHIP THROUGH MOVEMENT
A Guide for Establishing a Lifestyle of Worship

Published by Dawn Treader Publications
A ministry of Morning Star And Company, Inc.
2004

Unless otherwise indicated, Scripture quotations used in this book are from The Holy Bible, New International Version (NIV). Copyright © 1973, 1978, 1984 International Bible Society. Used by permission of Zondervan Bible Publishers. The King James Version of the Bible (KJV). New American Standard Bible® (NASB) © 1960, 1977, 1995 by the Lockman Foundation. Used by permission.

Throughout the write of this book there is no acknowledgement given to satan or the devil; wherever the name appears it is in lowercase.

For information:
DAWN TREADER PUBLICATIONS
POST OFFICE BOX 22175
BEACHWOOD, OHIO 44122
www.dawntreaderpublications.com

Library Of Congress Cataloging-In-Publication Data

Moore, Rachel L., 1967-
Rivers of praise worship through movement : a guide for establishing a lifestyle of worship
/ Rachel L. Moore ; foreword by Steve Sawyer.
    p. cm.
Includes bibliographical references and index.
ISBN 1-58993-075-4 (pbk. : alk. paper)
1. Worship programs. 2. Dance--Religious aspects--Christianity. I. Title.
BV198.M66 2004
248.3--dc22

                                                    2004013700
Printed in the United States of America
04 05 06 07 — 7 6 5 4 3 2 1 0

To my husband, Johnny and our three sons,
Jonathan, Jamicah, and Jeremy

From the Worship and Prophetic Community

"The Holy Spirit is releasing such materials at this time to prepare and build the third day church. [This book] inspires me and fed my spirit."

Apostle David Swan (Tan Suan Chew)
Author and Founding Pastor, Tabernacle of David
Kuala Lumpur, Malaysia

"The Lord is once again rebuilding the Tabernacle of David (Amos 9:11; Acts 15:16) and restoring His purpose for continual praise and worship in and through His people. Rachel Moore has been called and anointed to be one of those who are able to present these truths by instruction and demonstration.

She has thoroughly studied the Scriptures in regard to worship through movement and has been able to present her findings in a manner that is easily understood by the novice in worship as well as the skilled. The personal experiences she shares from her own life brings enthusiasm and confidence for the reader to step into new arenas of praise, worship and dance.

Rachel's prophetic mantle is evident and she has given herself as a vessel that demonstrates the heart of God in purity not only in her movement but also in the integrity of her life and ministry."

(Prophet) Jim and (Apostle) Judy Stevens
Christian International Board of Governors
CI International Regional Leaders
Marion Christian Center

"Randall Bane, a Christian movement artist had this to say in his article, *Raising a Standard*, 'Just as musicians learn to control their instruments, singers their voices, and preachers their deliveries, movement ministers must learn the skills appropriate to their calling. Whether through formal training or through applying self-discipline to a natural gift, they are called to do what all in ministry must do: glorify God and bring love and truth to mankind. Success is measured in fruit!' and I agree."

Rush Dillingham
Christian Movement Artist
Atlanta, Georgia

"The book deals with the purpose and benefits of an anointed dance ministry. It will explain the importance of the spiritual and physical preparation necessary for people to prepare themselves for the dance ministry. It will instruct you on the practical, as well as, the spiritual concept of how to start a dance ministry. Judah (Praise) will lead out, going into the enemy's camp and tearing down satan's kingdom."

Drs. David and Vernette Rosier
Founders and Pastors, Panama City Fellowship Church of Praise, Inc.
Apostolic Overseers, FCP Network of Covenant Churches and Ministries

"Paul speaks to us in 1 Corinthians 14:10, 11 (NKJV), 'There are, it may be, so many kinds of languages in the world, and none of them is without significance (meaning). Therefore, if I do not know the meaning of the language, I shall be a foreigner to him who speaks, and he who speaks will be a foreigner to me.'

Though Paul is referring to a discourse on speaking in our spiritual language, the fact remains that dance, too, is a language — a non-verbal language that has the ability to speak.

As worshipers, may we continue to spiritually and practically decode the language of dance, so that we might clearly communicate the greatest and most precious message of Truth known to the universe."

Reverend Yvonne D. Peters
Dance Director and Choreographer
Feast of Tabernacles, International Embassy, Jerusalem
Worship Watch Director, Christian Assembly, Columbus, Ohio

"I came from a traditional church and never thought of praising God through movement (only by singing and or praying), but after reading this book, I understand and agree that I can praise the Lord with my whole body moving. Setting time aside alone with the Lord each day has become a necessity — a key to cultivating intimacy with God.

This is a magnificent book! By reading it, the Lord will lift your heart in richer, more abundant praise and lead you to a greater intimacy with Him. You will come to realize that setting time aside alone with the Lord each day will become a necessity. It is key to cultivating intimacy with Him. You will understand that you can worship the Lord with your whole body in movement. This book is not targeted just for dancers, but for every individual who wants to develop greater intimacy with the Lord through movement."

Indriana Koo
Worshiper, Kathleen, Georgia, and Native from Indonesia

"The man who God called, "a man after His own heart" was a worshiper. However, notice that King David's harp playing and singing was appreciated by friend and foe (Saul), but his dancing was despised.

Wow . . . finally a book that removes the mystery and unveils this liberating gift of worship called dance. It emanates joy, fun, and freedom as you read. It creates curiosity and hunger for the Lord and a desire to worship Him more.

It encouraged me to stay consistent in my private worship time with the Lord."

Maureen VanEllison
Worshiper, Macon, Georgia

"God is always raising up someone who will yield and give Him glory. Rachel is a voice speaking to a wilderness saying the Kingdom of God is now! Let us worship Him with our whole heart in spirit, in truth, and in the beauty of holiness!"

Apostles James E. Blue, Jr. and Grace M. Blue
Cincinnati, Ohio

"It's high time that the Body of Christ takes seriously His call to 'worship Him in the dance.' Our generation cries out for the reality of His presence in His people. With the hunger for media, technology, etc., we have a great opportunity to display Jesus through the arts if we do this 'His way' and follow the leading of the Spirit of God.

Jesus wants more than an audience of hand-clappers; He wants us to gloriously pour out our hearts of worship and love to Him so that He, in turn, can shower the onlookers with <u>Himself</u> and His fullness."

Deborah K. Smith, Minister
Director, Beautiful Feet Christian Dance Center, Macon, Georgia
Leader, Vessels of Honor Worship Dance Team, Harvest Cathedral

"This book trains you in a more excellent way. Awesome for any and everyone!"

Barbara Wallace Erkins
Pastor, Eagle's Vision Christian Center
Author, By Any Other Name It's Still Sex

Acknowledgments

First, I dedicate this book back to God and thank Him for giving me the ability and inspiration to write.

I thank my wonderful, understanding husband Johnny, for giving me liberty to do things that God calls me to do. He has supported me in taking care of our three sons, Jonathan, Jamicah, and Jeremy while I spent hours studying and preparing the book.

I thank my publisher, editors, and all the support people on the Rivers Project. I thank Kim-Andréa Richardson for her unending support and encouragement.

I thank the Rivers of Praise prayer team for their continued support in prayer.

I thank my pastor, Steve Sawyer for supporting the book and our dance ministry at the church.

I thank Maureen Van Ellison for her support and comments in proofing the manuscript.

I thank all of the endorsers and reviewers for providing their much appreciated words of encouragement.

I thank all of the dancers who participated in the Rivers Project.

I thank Leon Seymore, Jr. for using his gift of music to help the development of the Rivers of Praise theme song.

I thank my husband, Johnny and Paul Talley for their beautiful photographs for this work.

I thank my natural parents, Henry and Carolyn Dickerson for giving me life and for their love and support throughout the years. I thank my mother Carolyn for her prayers.

I thank my spiritual parents, Drs. David and Vernette Rosier for laying a solid foundation of the Word in my life and for the prophetic words that kept me on God's purposed path.

I thank Pastors James and Grace Blue for allowing God to develop me and use me within the dance ministry of their church.

I thank the worshipers for whom this book is written. Your hunger and thirst for more resources on worship and dance ministry increased the intensity and inspiration of my writing.

Contents

Foreword   xv
Preface: Rivers of Praise, What Does It Mean?   xvii

SPIRITUAL ELEMENTS

1. The Pattern for Worship   1
2. The Word of God – Our Biblical Cord for Eternal Life   19
3. The Chambers of God – The Passageway of Faith   27
4. Secret Hiding Place – Prayer as a place of Refuge   35
5. Relationship with Christ – Developing an Intimate Connection with God   47
6. Cultivating the Heart – Attaining the Character of Christ   59
7. Praise Unlimited – Clothed with Spiritual Garments   77

APPLICATION ELEMENTS

1. The Word on Dance – The Ministry of Dance   89
2. Ministry Mission   101
3. Technical Methods for the Ministry of Dance   109
4. Spiritual Warfare and Winning Battles   119
5. Prophecy and Prophetic Dance   127
6. Teaching Your Fingers to War – Signing and Dance   147

PRACTICAL ELEMENTS

1. Organizing a Dance Team   153
2. Temple Maintenance   169
3. Choreography   173
4. Props for Praise   177
5. Priestly Garments to Fit You for the King   183
6. Empowering Youth to Worship God   189
7. Looking Ahead – The Ministering Arts in Evangelism   193

- **Notes of Encouragement**   197
- **About the Author**   198
- **Notes**   199
- **Glossary**   203

Foreword

We can't help it. God made us that way. We were born with the dance inside of us. First, we lay in our cribs and kicked our legs. Then as soon as we could pull up and hang onto the rails, we bobbed up and down to the music. And God liked it. In fact, He liked it so much He put it in the Book: "Let them praise His name in the dance..." (Ps. 149:3).

As believers we should all praise God for at least two reasons, because He likes it and because He told us to. But we have discovered so many more reasons to praise Him. We have discovered that praise changes everything! In fact, praise will alter the very atmosphere you and I live in.

In Ephesians 2:2 Paul called the devil the "prince of the power of the air (atmosphere)." The devil tries his best to control the atmosphere surrounding us, for he knows that the atmosphere around us will govern our lives. At any given time we are moving through life in an atmosphere of victory or defeat, of faith or unbelief, of confidence or doubt, of peace or fear.

Nothing changes that atmosphere more quickly or completely than Word-based praise. Psalm 22:3 tells us that God Himself inhabits, indeed He is enthroned upon the praises of His people. Praise immediately establishes the Lordship of Jesus in the face of our enemy. Praise also confuses and binds the enemy. Psalm 149:6-9 tells us that the one-two punch of the Word of God combined with the high praises of God "binds their kings with chains and their nobles with fetters of iron." It goes on to say that such praise causes the sentence of judgment to be executed against the enemy. It should be evident why the devil so despises praise.

Praise should flow like a mighty river through our lives, but often that river gets clogged up with debris. The debris might be criticism, the result of our trying to praise God with the same mouth that we use to speak critically and hateful of others. James asks, in 3:11, "Does a fountain send out from the same opening both fresh and bitter water?" The blockage might be sin, or it might be some of the dams that religious traditions have built.

Regardless, purpose in your heart today to experience the powerful river of praise flowing into and out of your life. This book can help you, because it teaches the heart of a worshiper, as well as the joy of dancing. Dance is such a powerful form of praise in that it encompasses the use of the whole body in worship.

Rachel Moore and her husband, Johnny, are wonderful people and faithful members of our church. The Lord has blessed Rachel beyond the ability to dance and worship; He has gifted her with a creative passion. I know her writing and ministry will bless you.

May this work cause you to pull up again, and dance to the music of His wonderful grace.

Steve Sawyer
Senior Pastor, Harvest Cathedral
Macon, Georgia

Rivers of Praise, What Does It Mean?

In 1991, God gave me a vision of many streams of color flowing out of a scarlet heart. Those streams of color represented rivers of praise. God desires that we worship Him in spirit and in truth. He desires pure praise to come forth from our hearts and out of our lips. The fruit of our lips will cause us to reap many blessings.

Not many months later, the vision manifested into a beautiful banner of brilliant rainbow colors. The banner represented a covenant relationship with Christ, and rivers of life filled with thanksgiving and praise flowing from a soft sincere scarlet heart. The gold surface of the banner was accented by seven green Hebrew words meaning praise – Yadah, Towdah, Halal, Tehillah, Zamar, Barak, and Shabach. The green symbolized life, growth, and prosperity, while the gold symbolized kingdom glory. Malachi 3:3-4 reads, *"He will sit as a refiner and purifier of silver; He will purify the Levites and refine them like gold and silver. Then the LORD will have men who will bring offerings in righteousness, and the offerings of Judah and Jerusalem will be acceptable to the LORD, as in days gone by, as in former years."* As we live before God, desiring to please Him in everything we say and do, He will refine us as pure gold. Our offerings of praise will come before Him as a sweet aroma. Our praises unto God are considered sacrifices as we crucify our flesh through submission. We are submitting our mind, our will, and our emotions unto God, being attentive to give Him praise. We sacrifice our feelings and circumstances, laying them on the altar to present our praise and thanksgiving unto our Lord.

Back to Eden

I began searching the scriptures to gain more understanding of my vision. So why not start in the book of Genesis where all things originated? Interesting enough, there it was in Eden, a well-watered garden. Eden is defined as pleasure and delight. God planted a garden eastward in Eden especially for His children's pleasure. The Garden of Eden was the first home of Adam and Eve, a place of fruitfulness and prosperity. Every tree that was pleasant to the eye and good for food grew in this garden. The *tree of the knowledge of good and evil* and the *tree of life* were also in the garden. Adam and Eve had free access to God and could commune with Him as much as their heart desired. The presence of God was with them. A river flowed out of Eden to water this special garden. There was so much beauty and life there. This river began in Eden, but then branched out into four major rivers.

The first river mentioned in Genesis 2:11 is the Pishon, which means to spread, to be scattered and to disperse. The Pishon flowed in a complete circle around the land of Havilah. The Hebrew term for Havilah is *chuwl*, meaning circular, to twist or whirl in a circular or spiral manner and to dance. The Pishon, a river of praise in action, had such movement that it caused the other rivers to spread out in their proper directions. Here we see a natural element moving in dance before the first mention of man dancing.

Let the rivers clap their hands, let the mountains sing together for joy
— Psalm 98:8

Psalm 148 declares, let all creation praise the Lord. One of the Hebrew words for praise is *machowl,* meaning a round dance. It is referenced in the book of Psalms in several places. The psalmist declares, "Let them praise His name in the dance" (Ps. 149:3), and "Praise Him with the timbrel and dance" (Ps. 150:4). The same type of dance is also referenced in Jeremiah 31:13 and Lamentations 5:15.

The second river, Gihon, was the river compassing Ethiopia. The root meaning of Gihon is a stream, a river of paradise. Gihon is also referenced from *giyach*, which means to gush forth, to draw up, to take out, and to labor bringing forth life. Solomon was anointed king over Israel at Gihon (I Kings 1:33). The last two rivers were Hiddekel, which is now called the Tigris, and the Euphrates, both have similar definitions, meaning to go forth or to break forth. All four rivers originating from Eden went throughout the earth to bring forth life, growth, and fruitfulness. So shall the Spirit of the Lord go forth throughout the earth to bring forth life, causing both righteousness and praise to spring up before all nations (Isa. 61:11).

Only a well-watered garden can yield desirable fruit. As believers we are planted in the garden of the Lord, we are watered by the Word and by His Spirit, which causes righteousness and praise to spring forth out of us. God desires praise to go before all nations of the earth. Why not allow praise to break forth from a constant source, the body of Christ, and disperse into the four corners of the earth just as the rivers from Eden? These rivers of praise flowing out of the body of Christ will bring forth life everywhere.

> They will come and shout for joy on the heights of Zion; they will rejoice in the bounty of the LORD — the grain, the new wine and the oil, the young of the flocks and herds. They will be like a well-watered garden, and they will sorrow no more. Then maidens will dance and be glad, young men and old as well. I will turn their mourning into gladness; I will give them comfort and joy instead of sorrow. I will satisfy the priests with abundance, and my people will be filled with my bounty," declares the LORD. — Jeremiah 31:12-14

Praise can be expressed in a variety of forms, just as bodies of water or rivers come in many shapes and sizes. The dictionary states, "a river is a natural stream of water of considerable volume; and a stream is a body of running water flowing on the earth, a steady succession of water, a constantly renewed supply, a continuous moving procession or an unbroken flow."[1] A stream also means to leave a bright trail. Likewise, there should be a continuous stream of praise flowing from our hearts and spirit unto our Lord and Savior Jesus Christ. That unbroken flow of praise will form streams of resilient colors, all declaring God's glory and grace. Our passionate praise will leave a bright trail for others to follow.

Spiritual Waters

The vision within Ezekiel 47:1-11 is symbolic of the Holy Spirit being a river with a constant life giving flow that comes from Jesus Christ. We individually represent the temple of the Holy Spirit. Here in Ezekiel the river filled the temple. The waters grew from ankle deep, to knee deep, to waist deep and then to overflow. We want the anointing of the Holy Spirit to fill our temple to the point of overflow. The Holy Spirit can flow in every area of our lives as we yield to a life of worship, a life of prayer, and a life of obedience in the Word.

> The man brought me back to the entrance of the temple, and **I saw water coming out from under the threshold of the temple** toward the east (for the temple faced east). The water was coming down from

under the south side of the temple, south of the altar. He then brought me out through the north gate and led me around the outside to the outer gate facing east, and the water was flowing from the south side. As the man went eastward with a measuring line in his hand, he measured off a thousand cubits and then led me through **water that was ankle-deep.** He measured off another thousand cubits and led me through **water that was knee-deep.** He measured off another thousand and led me through **water that was up to the waist.** He measured off another thousand, but **now it was a river that I could not cross, because the water had risen and was deep enough to swim in — a river that no one could cross.** He asked me, "Son of man, do you see this?" Then he led me back to the bank of the river. When I arrived there, I saw a great number of trees on each side of the river. He said to me, "This water flows toward the eastern region and goes down into the Arabah, where it enters the Sea. When it empties into the Sea, the water there becomes fresh. **Swarms of living creatures will live** wherever the river flows. There will be large numbers of fish, because this water flows there and makes the salt water fresh; so **where the river flows everything will live.** Fishermen will stand along the shore; from En Gedi to En Eglaim there will be places for spreading nets. The fish will be of many kinds-- like the fish of the Great Sea. But the swamps and marshes will not become fresh; they will be left for salt. **Fruit trees of all kinds will grow on both banks of the river. Their leaves will not wither, nor will their fruit fail.** Every month they will bear, because the water from the sanctuary flows to them. **Their fruit will serve for food and their leaves for healing.**" — Ezekiel 47:1-12

Pause for Prayer

Dear Lord, please help us to grow in Your Spirit to the point of overflow so that we might become those trees bearing lasting fruit. Allow Your Spirit to take us into the deep things of God so that we might experience the joy of being a blessing to others, having our fruit serve for food and our leaves for healing — "their fruit will serve for food and their leaves for healing."

The Apostle John reminds us that within every believer will flow streams of living water. "Whoever believes in Me, as the Scripture has said, streams of living water will flow from within him" (John 7:38). The living water from this verse represents life and the Holy Spirit flowing like a continuous fountain. We must allow the rivers of life to flow out of us. The life of the spirit shall bring forth praise unto the Most High God. When praise flows from our hearts, God can purge those things that are not like Christ, removing those things that are not pleasing to Him. Increasing our praise and worship time will allow the current of the Holy Spirit to move forcefully, purging those things right out of our inward man. Opening our mouths to give God thanks, declaring His mighty acts, lifting our hands, bowing before Him, singing, shouting, and dancing is like opening a dam, releasing the waters. These powerful waters will come forth like a flood. Even during the time of Noah when God released the waters from heaven to flood the earth, nothing could stand in its way. As we allow ourselves to be free, withholding nothing from the Lord, those rivers of life and those rivers of praise will flow out of us. Nothing will have the strength to stand in our way.

Praise is considering, declaring and extolling God for all that He has done, for all that He is doing, and for all that He will do. We must learn to take "time out" moments in our busy schedules just to praise and worship God. We don't necessarily have to be locked in a closet or room to praise Him. We can praise God while on the go, while driving the car, while in the kitchen, or while doing chores. We can even sing songs of praise while playing with the kids. God inhabits the praises of His people (Psalm 22:3), which means that God is right there with us, enjoying every moment, and stands ready to meet our needs.

King David gives a perfect example of how to extol God. We will glean from his lifestyle of worship later. Some of the words of King David are, "When I consider Your heavens, the work of Your fingers, the moon and the stars, which You have set in place; what is man that You are mindful of him, the son of man that You care for him? You made him a little lower than the heavenly beings and crowned him with glory and honor. You made him ruler over the works of your hands; you put everything under his feet: all flocks and herds, and the beasts of the field, the birds of the air, and the fish of the sea, all that swim the paths of the seas. O LORD, our Lord, how majestic is your name in all the earth!"[2]

In worship some may desire to be all alone with the Lord or at least undisturbed. A partial definition of worship is the acknowledgment of God, of His nature and attributes. In worship we bow "self" down to reverence and exalt God. We can worship God in word and in deed. We can worship Him by reciting the Word and calling out His attributes. For example, "You are the Lord of lords and King of kings, a God who forgives and delivers, and a God who loves and is full of patience, grace, and mercy."

We can worship God in deed, through a walk of obedience in every thing that we do. Walking in obedience is worshipping God. When we love according to I Corinthians 13, we are worshipping God. When we forgive those who have hurt us, we are worshipping God. Let's consider it a challenge and an honor to live a life of worship unto God. During the times alone with our Lord, praising and worshipping Him, our character will be challenged to mirror the character of Christ. We were also created with instruments for worship. Our bodies were designed to move and to respond. We have been clothed with garments of salvation and with a robe of righteousness. Let us rejoice in our Savior Jesus Christ, for who He is, and for all He has done. Later we will examine the process of developing godly character. We will also review the story of Lucifer and his lost position. Lucifer was created to worship God. His body was uniquely designed with instruments for worship.

We all have different ways of expressing our worship unto the Lord. However, we will learn throughout the chapters of this book that true worship goes beyond lifting hands, singing, dancing, and creating music with instruments. True worship is all about the heart. The attitudes of our heart can hinder pure worship and praise. Hence, it is necessary for the healing waters of the Spirit to purify our hearts, and out of a pure heart the rivers of praise will flow. Then as we individually allow praise to flow from our lips, from our song, and from our dance we will experience an overflow. A massive move of the Spirit will occur as the rivers of praise flow out of our spirit, overflowing onto hard places to make them soft again, pushing down bridges that divide, and uprooting anything that causes division. That which binds us can no longer hold us captive. Overflow is what causes dams to break. Nothing will be able to stand against this flood of the Spirit moving through praise. As this river flows through the Body of Christ, God will unite His people by His love. Then each river of praise will meet, converge, and overtake. The Body of Christ operating in unity will wreak havoc in the enemy's camp, causing the kingdom of darkness to be swallowed up in victory!

The end-time harvest will depend upon God's people operating in love, walking in unity and obedience, and lifting high the standard of the Word while magnifying and praising God.

Allow your praise to flow like a river—Rivers of Praise!

Now, let's explore the different elements of this book. The diagram below gives a visual layout of how each chapter is linked with a particular element. Listed first are the spiritual elements, all of which are foundational, aiding in the spiritual growth of any individual or ministry while giving instructional insight to developing a lifestyle of worship. The next two sections embrace both the application and practical elements that are essential for a ministry of worship through movement.

Rivers of Praise
Worship Through Movement

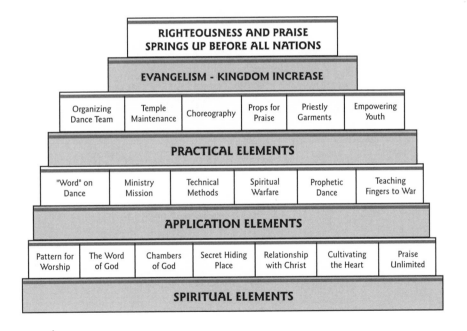

For as the soil makes the sprout come up and a garden causes seeds to grow,
so the Sovereign LORD will make righteousness and praise spring up before all nations.
— Isaiah 61:11

SPIRITUAL ELEMENTS

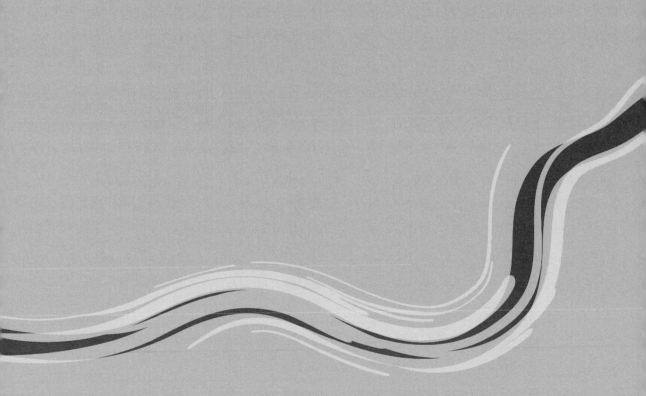

1: The Pattern for Worship

How should our lifestyle exemplify worship? Well, we were given a set of instructions for worship in the Old Testament and a set of different instructions for worship in the New Testament. In this chapter, we will begin with the old covenant law and progress through to the new covenant that was established by Jesus Christ.

The Old Testament is filled with terminology that provides us with symbols, types, and shadows of what was to come in the New Testament (Covenant). We can refer back to those things as a pattern to help guide us in our worship under the new covenant.

The waters that flowed from the temple in the vision of Ezekiel were symbolic of the Spirit of the Lord Jesus entering into the temple of our hearts. We are living out that vision under the new covenant through Jesus Christ. The waters grew to great heights until it became a river so deep that one would have to swim to get across it. This river brought life to everything it touched. The Spirit of the Lord in our temple has brought us life. The progressive increase of this river expresses the measure of the levels that God desires to increase in our lives. Our lifestyle of worship should continually increase as we grow in His likeness. From the moment that the Spirit of the Lord entered into the temple of our hearts, thanksgiving and praise began to flow. As God increases in us, worship and praise should automatically increase, forming Rivers of Praise that are released unto the Lord.

Some of the first patterns for worship and offering sacrifices to God are seen in the early books of the Bible. The books of Exodus through Numbers give an account of the Tabernacle of Moses. The Tabernacle of David or Solomon's Temple is defined in 2 Chronicles. As we study, we gain a greater understanding of worship. Both the

Tabernacle of Moses and the Temple of Solomon were considered a *sanctuary*, a holy place set apart to worship God. Although a complete study on the sanctuaries is beyond the scope of this book, I will reference certain scriptures and highlight the symbols pertinent to building a lifestyle of worship. Most importantly, we will spend concentrated thought on what took place during the establishment of the new order, while making comparison to the old. (You may refer to *Dancing into the Anointing* by Aimee Verduzco Kovacs, which gives more detail about the tabernacle and temple in the Old Testament.)

Beginning in Exodus chapters 25 through 31, we see the blueprint and instructions given to Moses for building the Tabernacle of the Congregation (or Tent of Meeting). God told Moses to make a request of the children of Israel to bring an offering, giving it with a willing heart of their own free will. They brought gold, silver, brass, royal fabrics, fine linens, animal fur, shittim wood, liquid oil, fine stones, and spices for anointing oil and sweet incense, all of which were used to build the tabernacle according to the patterns given by God. Instructions were also given as to who was to minister unto the Lord, along with the methods and frequency in offering up the sacrifices. Within the tabernacle were three significant places to where the priest had to proceed to offer the sacrifices: the Outer Court, the Holy Place or Inner Court, and the Holy of Holies.

God instructed Moses on how to take the sweet spices to make a perfume after the art of the apothecary (Exod. 30: 35). Apothecary relates to the pharmaceutical profession where compounds for medical purposes are prepared, thus Moses was being asked to prepare a holy fragrant healing ointment. He was then directed to put some of the healing ointment before the Testimony in the Tabernacle of the Congregation, where God would meet with him. The Ark of the Covenant is also referred to as the Ark of the Testimony, which was the only article of furniture located in the Holy of Holies, the place where God's presence would reside. This special ointment was hidden and kept behind the veil before the Ark of the Testimony. A new

As God increases in us, worship and praise should automatically increase, forming Rivers of Praise that are released unto the Lord.

covenant between God and man was made when the veil of the flesh of Jesus was torn by the stripes during the crucifixion. Thereafter, the sweet healing ointment that could only be found before the presence of God was made available to us through the blood of Jesus. Thus, the scripture says, "...by whose stripes ye were healed" (1 Pet. 2: 24). Every emotional or physical healing that we receive while in the divine presence will go before us as a witness, testifying that we have met or have been with God.

Moses spent a considerable amount of time with God on Mount Sinai. It was on Mount Sinai that God spoke to Moses and wrote the Ten Commandments. While Moses was on the mountain, the Israelites grew restless in their waiting. They began to break their covenant with God by making a golden calf to worship. When Moses returned from his forty days on the mountain, he was angered by what he saw. In his anger he threw the two tables of testimony that had the engraved commandments from God to the ground, breaking them into pieces. After receiving some explanations from Aaron in defense of the people, Moses asked the people, "Who is on the Lord's side? Let him come unto me." The sons of Levi gathered voluntarily to Moses side. From that act, the Lord blessed them, chose them, and gave them the opportunity to serve God in capacities in which no other Israelite would have.

Moses was diligent in seeking the Lord. He met with God often. There was a spectacular after-glow upon the face of Moses because of his time spent with God while on Mount Sinai. The day came for God to make new tables for the commandments. Once again, God asked Moses to return to Mount Sinai so that the tables of the testimony could be rewritten. Moses learned that the Lord was merciful, gracious, longsuffering, and abundant in goodness and truth (Exod. 34:6). Moses reverenced God and worshipped Him in His awesomeness.

After receiving all of the instructions, the time came for the actual construction to take place. The hearts of the people were stirred in wisdom and they brought their freewill offering unto the Lord for the work of the tabernacle (Exod. 35:21). As we continue to read in Exodus 39:32, we find that all of the work to build the tabernacle was finally finished. The holy garments for the priest and servants were then designed (we will discuss this in detail in the "Priestly Garments" chapter). All things were set according to God's command and the tabernacle was ready to be erected and anointed (Exod. 40).

Remember the sons of Levi who rallied together with Moses? Well, it was now time for them to receive the blessing. Aaron and his sons were anointed and sanctified to serve in the office of high priest. The high priest offered the burnt offerings annually for themselves and for the sins of the people. They also led the people in worship and confession on a regular basis. All of the other Levites were set apart to serve as priests in the keeping of the sanctuary and to assist the high priest in preparing to minister unto the Lord. The Levites were charged to clean, to guard, and to transport the tabernacle.

As soon as the tabernacle was erected, something amazing happened. A cloud covered the tent of the congregation, and the glory of the Lord filled the tabernacle (Exod. 40:34). The glory of God was seen as a cloud in daylight and as a pillar of fire at night. Hence, the cloud signified to the people that God's presence was over the tabernacle. The tabernacle was portable and was moved wherever the children of Israel traveled. During those times when the cloud was seen, they could not journey nor move the tabernacle. They could only journey when the presence of God had lifted.

Throughout Leviticus, different types of offerings are defined. They were the trespass offering, burnt offering, meat offering, sin offering, peace offering, which is a sacrifice of thanksgiving type offering, the heave offering, vow or freewill offering, and wave offerings. All of these were offered on the *altar*. In the Outer Court, the *brazen altar* was used to offer blood sacrifices for the atonement of sin. First, in order for the sacrifice to be acceptable to God, there had to be blood shed. The blood was shed in the Outer Court by the door of the Tabernacle. The blood was poured beside the bottom of the *altar* and sprinkled around about the *altar*. The blood was also sprinkled on the *mercy seat* in the Most Holy Place.

A large curtain or *veil* separated the Holy Place from the Most Holy Place, which kept the Ark of the Covenant and the *mercy seat* out of reach. In the construction of the *mercy seat* were two cherubim, one at each end. The cherubim's wings spread out covering the *mercy seat*. The *mercy seat* stayed upon the Ark of the Covenant, and represented God's presence. God told Moses that He would meet and commune with him from above the *mercy seat*, from between the two cherubim (Exod. 25:22). Moses heard the voice of

God speaking to him from the *mercy seat* that was upon the Ark of Testimony, from between the two cherubim (Num. 7:89).

Another article found within the tabernacle was the *brazen laver* or *bronze basin* where the priest washed their hands and feet before entering into the sanctuary to minister unto God. The washing hands and feet was a part of the sanctification process and was required before offering the sacrifices before the Lord. There were other articles within the tabernacle such as the *altar of incense* (for burning fragrant incense), the *lamp stands* (for burning oil), and the *table of shewbread*.

It is important that we not become stuck under the old covenant. We must move forward in understanding the new covenant. We are to refer back to the old covenant as a pattern or as an example. Those things that were of the Old Testament law that were not changed in the New Testament still hold to be solid and true, such as the Ten Commandments. Jesus did not change the order of those things when He came to us.

We can compare the articles of the tabernacle to our lives under the new covenant. All of the articles are symbolic and are relevant to us today. First, there is the anointing oil that was used to anoint the tabernacle and all that was therein, which is symbolic of the Holy Spirit, the anointing of Jesus, the Anointed One (the Christ). The *brazen altar* where the blood of the sacrifices was shed is symbolic of the blood of Jesus Christ, who made atonement for our sin. It is also symbolic of us offering ourselves as a free will offering unto the Lord, a living sacrifice that is holy and acceptable unto Him. The *brazen laver* containing the water for washing is symbolic of the Word of God and the Holy Spirit. The pure water of the Word through the Spirit of the Lord can wash our minds clean. The *fragrant incense* is symbolic of our prayers, intercession, praise, and worship. The *lamp stand* that burned with oil is symbolic of the light of the Word of God that guides and enlightens the understanding of the believer. It also represents the believer being filled with the Holy Spirit. Our spirits are fed by the Word of God so that we might shine as a light for others to see Him. The *shewbread* symbolizes God's provision for those who serve Him, including our dependence for His provision, our daily bread. The *shewbread* represents need and dependence on the bread of life, which is the Word of God. We must feed our spirit with the Word in order to grow in the spirit.

King David and his son Solomon were the last two kings to reign over all of Israel (all twelve tribes together). They were considered righteous kings during their reign because they kept their covenant with God and did not lead the people away from God. Rehoboam, the son of Solomon caused the kingdom to split into two, Israel and Judah (2 Chron. 10). Hundreds of years passed before another righteous king came along to reign over Judah. King Asa was the next king that turned the people back towards God. He entered into a covenant with them to seek the Lord with all their heart and with all their soul (2 Chron. 15:12, 15). King Asa then removed his mother from her position as queen because of her idolatry. He cut down the wooden image, broke it into pieces, and burned it by the Brook Kidron.

The next righteous king to reign over Judah was King Hezekiah. Whenever there was an unrighteous king ruling over the house of Judah, the temple or sanctuary would be neglected and dust would collect on everything. King Hezekiah ordered the priest to come and clean the house of the Lord. They first sanctified themselves, and then went into the inner part of the house of the Lord. They brought out all of the uncleanness that was found in the temple. Then they took all that they had found to the Brook Kidron. There are additional scriptures that mention the Brook Kidron. In these scriptures, the Brook Kidron is referred to either passing over toward the way of the wilderness or death, a place to cast destroyed idols, or a place to cast dust or unclean things.

The last scripture that addresses the Brook Kidron is Jeremiah 31:40. Jeremiah prophesied the word of the Lord concerning the new covenant that Jesus would establish with His people. *"Behold, the days come, says the LORD, that I will make a new covenant with the house of Israel, and with the house of Judah: Not according to the covenant that I made with their fathers in the day that I took them by the hand to bring them out of the land of Egypt; which my covenant they brake, although I was an husband unto them, says the LORD:* **But this shall be the covenant that I will make with the house of Israel; After those days, says the LORD, I will put my law in their inward parts, and write it in their hearts; and will be their God, and they shall be my people.** *And they shall teach no more every man his neighbor, and every man his brother, saying, Know the LORD: for they shall all know me, from the least of them unto the greatest of them, says the LORD: for I will forgive their iniquity, and I will remember their sin no more."*[1] Make a mental note of this scripture because we will see this again later. At the very end of the prophecy in verse 40, the Brook Kidron is mentioned and Jeremiah declares that once the prophecy is fulfilled, the valley and the fields up to the Brook Kidron would be holy unto the Lord. We can see that Kidron definitely has spiritual significance for us, so let's proceed to the definition.

Nelson's Illustrated Bible Dictionary defines Kidron as a valley on the eastern slope of Jerusalem. Through that valley runs the Brook Kidron. During the winter, a tumultuous outpouring of rain occurs and during the summer months, the brook almost dries up completely. The ravine of the valley that was formed by the waters begins north of Jerusalem, running past the temple, Calvary, the Garden of Gethsemane, and the Mount of Olives to the eastern side of Jerusalem. From there, the valley and the brook reach into the Judean wilderness, and finally its course brings it to the Dead Sea. "The Dead Sea is called the Salt Sea at the lowest part of the earth. There is a large peninsula known as El-Lisan (**the Tongue**) that protrudes into the sea from the southeast shore. Throughout the centuries, this tongue separated the sea into two parts with a channel of water flowing between them on the west. From the depths of the northeast corner, the bottom of the sea quickly shelves and rises southward. Thus the area of the **sea south of El-Lisan is extremely shallow**."[2]

There are several things I would like to point out in this definition. The Brook Kidron runs into the Dead Sea. It is interesting that the peninsula that protrudes into the sea is called the tongue. Just like El-Lisan, our tongue can cause division if the wrong things are spoken from a heart that is filled with things that God wants dead in our lives. God wants those things that are not like Him to die and He wants us healed.

The Dead Sea is known for its beneficial effects on disease and within its waters is found some of the richest mineral and salt deposits on earth. Even now in the 21st century, people still go to the Dead Sea to soak their diseased bodies in the water. There is healing in the dying process of self. When we die to something that affects us negatively, we will know we are healed when the same triggers don't cause the usual response. We know we are healed when it doesn't hurt us anymore. The pain is gone.

The Levite priest took the unclean things from within the

sanctuary and took them to the Brook Kidron. God wants all of the uncleanness within the sanctuary of our hearts to be dead. Jesus prayed just before crossing over the Brook Kidron (Cedron) and entering into the garden of Gethsemane (John 17, 18:1). In His prayer He asked the Father to "sanctify us through His truth, thy word is truth" (John 17:17). Jesus Christ had to cross over the Kidron for His crucifixion. What a picture that paints for us. Jesus battled with His will; He died to His will and proceeded to His death because of the will of the Father. We must crucify our flesh by dying to self. We must die to certain things and embrace God's way.

We can compare the articles of the tabernacle to our lives under the new covenant.

The last point that I would like to highlight about the Brook Kidron is that a spring of the Gihon River that flowed out of Eden, flows on one side of the Brook Kidron.

Hebrews chapters seven to ten describe and compare the old covenant to the new. The Levitical priesthood was established under the Law of Moses. Jesus Christ annulled the law for priesthood when he offered Himself as the ultimate sacrifice, dying as a sin offering for all. Years before Israel (Jacob), his twelve sons, and even before his father Isaac, God sent a high priest to bless the house of Abraham. Abraham was blessed by King Melchizedek, a priest of the Most High God. At that moment the order of priesthood changed. It did not come into effect, however, until Jesus stepped in as high priest. Thereafter, the Priesthood was established after the order of Melchizedek. With the new priesthood a new law was given. The Lord Jesus, who is also a descendant from our father Abraham, descended from Judah, another tribe of Israel. The tribe of Judah never served as priest under the old law, but things changed when Jesus became the High Priest. The name *Judah* literally means praise. Those who come to praise the Lord are a part of the royal priesthood. All worshipers of Jesus Christ are priests under the new covenant.

As we read further, we see that Jesus has an unchangeable priesthood with a better testament that will continue forever. Jesus, our High Priest, is holy, harmless, undefiled, separate from sinners, and made higher than the heavens. Jesus sits on the right hand of the throne of the Majesty in the heavens. The neat thing about all of this is that, *the perfect tabernacle or sanctuary that Jesus entered is heaven itself!* Jesus went to heaven to appear for us in God's presence.

> For Christ did not enter a man-made sanctuary that was only a copy of the true one; he entered heaven itself, now to appear for us in God's presence. — Hebrews 9:24

If we look deeper into this scripture, we can see that the sanctuaries that were built by Moses and Solomon were mere copies of what was already in heaven. We have been given a picture of heaven; by looking at the numerous details given for the building of those sanctuaries, we can almost see the glorious Kingdom. Ezekiel and John both had visions of that heavenly place. There, the veil that separated man from the presence of God was destroyed. Thus, we gained access to the divine presence through the veil being destroyed, which is the body of Christ. We can now have confidence to enter the Most Holy Place by His blood.

Jesus came to do the will of the Father. Through His obedience, Jesus obtained a more excellent ministry. He is the mediator of the new covenant promises. The Lord spoke these words to be the new covenant, "*I will put my laws into their mind, and write them in their hearts; and I will be to them a God, and they shall be to me a people.*" These exact words were prophesied by Prophet Jeremiah stated earlier in this chapter. The prophecy was now fulfilled. All of those other sacrifices that were mentioned earlier became obsolete, being replaced by the new blood covenant of Jesus Christ, which is also the law of grace. However, those things did transition from the physical to the spiritual. It is by the spirit that the blood of Jesus covers our sins. It is through the spirit, by which the Spirit of Christ entered into our hearts. It is by the spirit that the laws of God enter the sanctuary of our hearts through reading the Word of God. The only type of sacrifice God cares about now is *how we present our lives before Him*, whether it is in praise to Him and obedience to His commandments. Psalm 51: 17 defines the sacrifices of God to be a broken spirit, a broken and a contrite heart. Contrite means to break into pieces, to humble, and to crush. God is pleased with a humbled heart. Remember how King Asa broke into pieces the idol of his mother? Well, anything that is within our hearts that does not represent Jesus must be destroyed and broken into pieces.

God has taken us beyond the point of the veil to where He desires to deal with our hearts. God desires to unveil the truth within the sanctuary of our hearts so that we can see truth and gain understanding. He wants to put His law in our minds and write them upon our hearts so that we can experience a new level of intimacy. The most intimate level of worship occurs within the secret chambers of our hearts when God is dealing with us. These are the true worshipers the Father seeks, those who will allow Him to write upon their hearts so that they see truth, become broken, and are changed, thereafter worshipping Him in spirit and in truth (John 4:23). God desires to take His bride to a new level of intimacy and worship.

We are to present our bodies as living sacrifices, holy, acceptable unto God, which is our reasonable service (Rom.12:1). The gifts and sacrifices that were offered under the Levitical order were not able to clear the conscience of the worshiper. On the contrary, when Jesus entered the perfect tabernacle by the shedding of His own blood, He obtained forgiveness for sin and eternal redemption for us. It is by the spirit, that the blood of Jesus cleanses our conscience. With all of that being said, "*Let us draw near to God with a pure heart in full assurance of faith, having our hearts sprinkled to cleanse us from a guilty conscience, and having our bodies washed with pure water. And let us consider how we may spur one another on toward love and good deeds.*"[3]

So, what should the new covenant worship look like under our High Priest Jesus Christ? Well, it all begins with us drawing near to God. We are to give praise to God and worship Him. We are to seek His face and His heart. We draw near to God so that our heart, mind, and body can be cleansed. The blood of Jesus was shed so that our hearts could be sprinkled from a guilty conscience. We don't have to feel guilty about things we struggle with when we submit them under the blood of Jesus. God wants our hearts pure. We will discuss that in detail later. Now, let's consider how we might encourage others towards love and good deeds, which is also a part of new covenant worship. God is not only looking at our hearts, but He wants us to consider our ways. He wants us to look at how we treat others. Are we doing things that will cause others to be drawn to God and His love so that they are inspired to do good? The Pharisees challenged Jesus asking Him which commandments He weighed the greatest. He answered them by saying that if they were to weigh any of them, he would weigh the first two commandments equally. The first states that we are to love the Lord our God with all our heart, with all our soul, and with our entire mind. Secondly, we are to love our neighbor as ourselves (Matt. 22:32-40)

Remember, the Levitical priest had to guard the gates of the sanctuary and they had to clean and maintain the sanctuary. We, the worshipers of Jesus are the priests after the new order, and have been given the same charge. We are to guard the gates to the sanctuary of our hearts and we are to clean and maintain that sanctuary. The result will be a pure heart. We will study this in more detail in the chapter, "Cultivating the Heart." We will also gain a better understanding of how the sanctuary of our heart is cleansed by the Spirit. Under the law of grace, there is no condemnation, but God does require us to carry out our priestly duties.

A Royal Priesthood

The royal priesthood exists because Jesus destroyed the veil that separated God's people from Him through the shedding of His own blood. Jesus consecrated us by destroying the veil of His own flesh, and giving His life as atonement for our sin. Divine healing was made available to us at that very moment. In addition, we became a chosen people under a new order, a royal priesthood, and a holy nation. Now as priest, we can go before the living God to present our sacrifices of praise without any inhibitions. We are to offer up our sacrifices of praise unto God, laying everything aside to worship Him. The Father sees the blood of His son Jesus in our place, flowing as a continuous stream of righteousness, holiness, and sanctification. We inherited the righteousness of Jesus Christ. Our covenant with Jesus gives us the right to the throne of grace where we receive mercy and forgiveness. We can enter God's presence without the fear of being destroyed. However, we must die to self. Our fleshly desires are consumed in the fire of His holy presence. The sanctuary of our heart is sprinkled with the blood of Jesus to free us from guilt. God promised to put His laws into our hearts and to write them in our minds. He promised this because His home is in our heart. Our heart became the new home of His Holy Spirit once we accepted Him as Savior. Jesus wants to clean house by His Spirit. He literally cleaned house when He cleaned the temple of the money changers. He cleaned that which was foreign and unacceptable.

We do not want to offer strange fire to God like the sons of Aaron (Lev. 10:1, Num. 3:4). **Strange fire represents something that is foreign or profane**. Oddly enough, *strange* here also means to commit adultery.[4] Those things that are foreign are like idols that must be destroyed. Anytime the Israelites had an idol, they committed adultery against God. They placed the idol in the place of God and their hearts were influenced by the wrong thing. We must allow God to purify our hearts and avoid offering praise and worship that is profane. Offering unholy fire occurs when our heart, motive, or life is not right. God wants our hearts to be cleansed, our minds to be renewed, and our ways towards others to be of a good report. He wants our entire bodies to be washed with "pure water." Now, how do you suppose we will get this inside, outside cleaning? This question will be answered throughout the course of this book.

Having therefore, brethren, boldness to enter into the holiest by the blood of Jesus, By a new and living way, which he hath consecrated for us, through the veil, that is to say, his flesh; And having an high priest over the house of God; Let us draw near with a true heart in full assurance of faith, having our hearts sprinkled from an evil conscience, and our bodies washed with pure water.
— Hebrews 10:19-22

My dear children, I write this to you so that you will not sin. But if anybody does sin, we have one who speaks to the Father in our defense-- Jesus Christ, the Righteous One. He is the atoning sacrifice for our sins, and not only for ours but also for the sins of the whole world. — 1 John 2:1-2

But you are a chosen people, a royal priesthood, a holy nation, a people belonging to God, that you may declare the praises of him who called you out of darkness into his wonderful light. Once you were not a people, but now you are the people of God; once you had not received mercy, but now you have received mercy. — 1 Peter 2:9-10

As you come to him, the living Stone-- rejected by men but chosen by God and precious to him-- you also, like living stones, are being built into a spiritual house to be a holy priesthood, offering spiritual sacrifices acceptable to God through Jesus Christ. — 1 Peter 2:4-5

There remains a veil; the veil of our flesh can limit our personal experiences with God. We must learn to deny our flesh. We are to be led by the Spirit and not by our flesh. Indulging ourselves in the perverse things of this world goes against this principal. Doing things "our way" rather than asking God for guidance goes against being led by the Spirit. As priest of the temple of the Holy Spirit, we must guard our hearts, our minds, our eyes, our ears, and our tongue. We must guard the gates to the sanctuary of our hearts, for they can either feed our flesh or feed our spirit. Leading a life in the Word of God, partnered with prayer, praise, and righteous living is a sure way to overcome the veil of the flesh. This combination will propel us to reach the heights in God that our hearts desire. Jude 21 tells us to keep ourselves in God's love as we wait for the mercy of our Lord Jesus Christ to bring us to eternal life. There is no need to walk in a fear of failing God, since Jesus is able to keep us and present us blameless before the presence of His glory. God is merciful and gracious towards anyone who draws near to Him.

Symbols of Significance

In carrying out our priestly duties, let's reflect on some of the symbols that are meant to be a pattern. Blood and water are mentioned together in the scriptures. Both water and blood were required before the priest entered the sanctuary. Just the same, Jesus came to us by water and blood. When a soldier pierced Jesus in the side during the crucifixion, blood and water flowed out together (John 19:34, 1 John 5:6-8).

The significance of the *brazen altar* to us is the blood of Jesus for atonement and the *brazen laver* with the water for cleansing. The blood of Jesus covers our sin and His Spirit cleanses our heart. However, we must remember to clean ourselves through repentance, reconciliation (getting things right with our brother), and washing ourselves in the Word of God.

The priest of old washed their hands and feet before offering sacrifices. That sets a good example for us to follow, since we are a part of the royal priesthood under Jesus, the High Priest (1 Pet. 2:5). We are instructed to cleanse our heart and our hands. We are to cleanse ourselves before offering our gifts and sacrifices of praise unto the Lord. A spiritual washing occurs through the act of repentance, reconciliation, and through the pure water of the Word. Matthew 5:24 and 25 reminds us that we should be reconciled with our brother before offering our gift at the altar. This is not to say that we are to lay our gift down and not be productive while we wait for God to perfect our hearts. This scripture addresses the process of reconciliation. We model the washing of our hands through reconciliation and making things right with those whom we have offended. We should never be the person who is holding up the reconciliation from occurring. We are to live at peace with all people. Therefore, we should humble ourselves and initiate reconciliation. Our hands are being washed of the situation as we take the appropriate steps to make things right with our brother. If the person chooses not to receive us or to forgive us, we are still free. Our conscience is clear because we have taken the appropriate steps to become reconciled. The peace of God will be our confirmation. As Psalm 26:6 and 7 says, "I wash my hands in innocence, and go about your altar, O LORD, proclaiming aloud your praise and telling of all your wonderful deeds." There should be nothing there to inhibit our praise. Many times through the process of reconciliation a part of our flesh dies. Pride diminishes while love and humility increase. We cannot afford any hindrance while offering our gifts to God. The washing of our feet is about our walk, our lifestyle. Is our walk clean before God? Are we considering our ways?

Therefore, if you are offering your gift at the altar and there remember that your brother has something against you; leave your gift there in front of the altar. First go and be reconciled to your brother; then come and offer your gift. — Matthew 5:23-24

It is true that we are to enter His gates with thanksgiving and into His courts with praise. We can literally offer our entire body as a sacrifice of praise through physical movements that reverence God during worship. The ministry of dance is another way of offering our entire body as a sacrifice of praise. Thanksgiving, praise, and obedience to God are all spiritual acts of worship, but we must not stop there, we must continue into that place of intimacy with God where He is speaking to our hearts and revealing secrets. That place of intimacy involves us being transformed into His character. God desires to mature us to love.

Another form of washing actively occurs through the written or spoken Word. Ephesians 5:26 tells us that we are sanctified and cleansed with the washing of water by the Word of God. As we meditate on the Word of God our minds are cleansed, purified, and renewed. Therefore, as we walk out and obey the Word of God, our lives are being sanctified and cleansed. God wants us to offer our mind, will, and emotions over to Him. If we want a renewed mind, then we must follow God's divine pattern. If we want to stand in His holy place to worship, we must cleanse our hands and purify our hearts.

Who may ascend the hill of the LORD? Who may stand in his holy place? He who has clean hands and a pure heart, who does not lift up his soul to an idol or swear by what is false, he will receive blessing from the LORD and vindication from God his Savior. — Psalm 24:3-5

We can literally offer our entire body as a sacrifice of praise through physical movements that reverence God during worship. The ministry of dance is another way of offering our entire body as a sacrifice of praise.

Now, let's discuss the last articles mentioned earlier in this chapter. The *fragrant incense* is symbolic of prayer, intercession, praise, and worship. Incense is referenced in Strong's Concordance as *qatar*.[5] *Qatar* means fumigation, a sweet incense or perfume; to smoke, that is to turn into fragrance by fire especially as an act of worship; to burn incense, to offer incense as a sacrifice.

As an act of worship, the priest of old burned sacrifices and incense to kindle a sweet smell of perfume before God. The sweet smell fumigated the atmosphere and God was pleased. Likewise, our praise, worship, and intercession create fragrance that is pleasing to God. We are to offer these type sacrifices on a continual basis. Daily, we can use our mouths to bless God with praise and thanksgiving. As the Psalmist declares in Psalm 34:1, "I will bless the Lord at all times. His praise shall continually be in my mouth."

> Through Jesus, therefore, let us continually offer to God a sacrifice of praise—the fruit of lips that confess his name.
> — Hebrews 13:15

Intercession is a spiritual sacrifice that approaches the throne as incense. An unselfish act delights God's heart. It is prayer on behalf of someone else, standing in the gap for a friend, loved one, or even for a nation. 1 Timothy 2:8 encourages the church to pray lifting up holy hands. A prayer that incorporates the movement of raising the arms and hands above the head is an expression of praise.

> Let my prayer be set forth before thee as incense; and the lifting up of my hands as the evening sacrifice.
> — Psalm 141:2

Obedience is the last spiritual sacrifice I would like to mention. 1 Samuel 15:22 reminds us, "to obey is better than sacrifice." Obedience in our daily lives is a spiritual sacrifice that God esteems highly over any other sacrifice.

Now, what about the symbol of the *lamp stand*? The lamps

were filled on a continuous basis with pure oil of crushed olives. The oil is symbolic of the anointing and the Holy Spirit. We all want the anointing to be evident in our lives. There is a price that each of us must pay to acquire that continuous flow of the anointing. We will be crushed by different circumstances that come as trials of life. Though our souls are crushed, God is aiming for the anointing. He is the only one who knows how to draw it out of us. Moses poured the anointing oil upon Aaron's head to anoint and consecrate him (Lev. 8:12). God anoints, consecrates, and sets us apart for the work to which He has called us. The Holy Spirit is the anointing of God. He is our comforter, our helper, our teacher, our partner, and our guide. Just as the lamps on the *lamp stand* provided light, He will light the path for us. The Holy Spirit will shine in us to expel darkness and reveal truth. He will also shine through us to light a path for others to follow.

The spiritual significance of the articles within the tabernacle can and should be applied to our every day lives. The instructions given for the preparation and construction of the Tabernacle of Moses were thorough. They not only included what was needed and what was to be done in constructing the Tabernacle, but also included the types of offerings that were acceptable to the Lord. When the time came for Solomon to build the Temple, a pattern already existed. God gave Solomon wisdom as to how he could build the temple on behalf of his father David. The Temple of Solomon is discussed in its entirety within the first five chapters of 2 Chronicles. We see that the work of building the temple was completed in chapter five, and every article and holy vessel that was in the Tabernacle of Moses were brought into Solomon's Temple. The priest then brought the Ark of the Covenant into its new home in the Most Holy Place.

Once the priests were out of the holy place, they began to praise the Lord. The priests consisted of three Levitical families, Asaph, Heman, and Jeduthun. These

A prayer that incorporates the movement of raising the arms and hands above the head is an expression of praise.

family names fit their jobs perfectly. Asaph means Jehovah has gathered, Heman means faithful, and Jeduthun relates to expressing praise. When those terms are adjoined, we have, "Jehovah God has gathered the faithful to express praise unto Him." Isn't that awesome? Those family names are listed in that order in 2 Chronicles 5:12. Likewise, God is gathering the faithful worshipers to Himself to express praise to His name. As members of the royal priesthood under the High Priest, Jesus Christ, we should express praise unto Him in every way that we can.

A life that contains the substance of the articles listed inside the sanctuary will reflect a lifestyle of worship. The sanctuary of our hearts should contain the Holy Spirit, the Word of God, prayers of intercession, and praise. However, we must remember that keeping our hearts before God, keeping our minds on God, and keeping our acts about God, are all considered worship, and were emphasized under the new covenant. In the next few chapters, we will study the details of the various elements that are essential in developing a lifestyle of worship.

2: The Word God
Our Biblical Cord to Eternal Life

God desires that we become like that well-watered garden in Eden. He desires that we become beautiful, delightful, fruitful, and prosperous. So, what are the things that must flow into the sanctuary of our hearts to promote our spiritual growth? We will explore these spiritual streams throughout the "Spiritual Elements" chapters. As we progress, we will see how each element flows together to make one beautiful in the Lord.

The Apostle John wrote in Revelations 22:1 that the angel showed him the river of the water of life flowing from the throne of God. Jesus said that He is the River of life. In John 4:13-14, Jesus answered the woman at the well saying, *"Everyone who drinks this water will be thirsty again, but whoever drinks the water I give him will never thirst. Indeed, the water I give him will become in him a spring of water welling up to eternal life."* In other words, Jesus was telling her that He wanted to give her His Spirit so that the river of life could flow through her. He wanted her to partake of His Spirit so that she could become one of the worshipers that the Father seeks after (John 4:23-24). Those who worship the Father in spirit and truth will be the true worshipers. As believers in the Lord Jesus Christ, the Spirit of Christ lives within us, giving us the ability to worship in spirit. But how do we worship the Father in truth? We must first know the Truth. The gospel of Jesus Christ is the Word of Truth; and the Word of Truth is the Word of God. The Word of God in us will become a river welling up inside bringing forth life and eternal prosperity.

The Word of God is the main source of our spiritual growth. According to Colossians 1:6, **the gospel bears fruit and grows in**

A rhema (Greek) is a word or an illustration God speaks directly to us, and it addresses our personal, particular situation.[6]

those who hear and understand its truth. Therefore, in order for us to experience spiritual fruit growing in our lives, we must stay connected to the source. In the beginning was the Word and the Word was with God and the Word was God (John 1:13). The Word is "a theological phrase which expresses the absolute, eternal, and ultimate being of Jesus Christ."[1] The Word, Jesus Christ became flesh and dwelt among mankind (John 1:14). Those who had the opportunity to see Jesus in the flesh had the advantage of learning His teaching first hand. We now have the opportunity to learn of His teachings by reading the *logos*, which is the written Word of God. Reading and studying the Bible helps us build our relationship with our Savior. It also helps us grow in the way of righteousness. Through God's Word, He shows His love for us, imparts His will to us, shares His heart with us, and reveals His plans for us. Whenever the written Word speaks to our personal situations, it becomes a *rhema*. The Word is life and it becomes the living Word. It is as if Jesus Himself was speaking directly to our personal situation (1 John 1:1-3).

Not only did God give us the written Word, but He also gave us His Spirit, the Holy Spirit, to assist us in our spiritual growth (John 14:26). The Holy Spirit enlightens our understanding of the Bible as we read, meditate, and study. He helps us to remember the Word so that we may apply it to our life situations at the appropriate times. We also learn by His Spirit, more about the person, Jesus Christ, and His great love for all mankind.

As newborn babes, we are instructed to desire the sincere milk of the Word so that we might grow in our understanding of God (1 Pet. 2:2). The milk of the Word is the foundational principle of the Word of God such as understanding love, repentance from dead works, water baptism, Holy Spirit baptism, communion, stewardship, and so forth. Feasting on the Word brings life. Feasting on the Word of God is essential to our spiritual growth.

Therefore let us leave the elementary teachings

about Christ and go on to maturity, not laying again the foundation of repentance from acts that lead to death, and of faith in God, instruction about baptisms, the laying on of hands, the resurrection of the dead, and eternal judgment. And God permitting, we will do so.

— Hebrews 6:1-3

If God were to open our eyes so that we could see how we looked in our spiritual development, we would be in for a rude awakening. We would see more babies walking around than the mature. The Apostle Paul said it so well when he spoke to those whom he had taught the Word. Apostle Paul was disappointed to find that many were spiritually immature. They were still unskillful in the Word and still needed to be taught the basic principles of God's Word. *"For when for the time ye ought to be teachers, ye have need that one teach you again which be the first principles of the oracles of God; and are become such as have need of milk, and not of strong meat. For every one that used milk is unskillful in the word of righteousness: for he is a babe."*[2] The Apostle Paul actually called them babies. We don't want to be caught wearing diapers, still requiring the milk of the Word in order to survive when we are to be the teachers to the new borne babes in Christ. When the Word is being taught, it is intended to invoke us to want more; it is intended to invoke us to seek God for more understanding and application.

In order for spiritual growth to occur, we must learn to study and meditate on the Word. Meditating is to mentally reflect on God and His works.[3] It is reflecting on His precepts, promises, and instructions.[4] Meditating is like chewing before swallowing and then digesting. The only way to get the nutrients out of our natural foods is through the digestive system. Without certain nutrients, healthy development of the body would not be possible. Likewise, we need to digest the Word so that the spiritual nutrients will promote spiritual growth. Reflecting on specific scriptures helps to break down a particular text or subject, which gives us the ability to digest it better. Most of the time when we read the Bible as our daily devotional duties, we really just scan the scriptures. We may not have even understood what we read. It becomes easier to understand a scripture if when we study we take a little at a time, and dissect it piece by piece. As we are taught the Word, we grow in knowledge. As we study and meditate on the Word, we expand our knowledge and understanding. As we apply the knowledge and understanding from the Word, we mature. The Word will become part of us, providing the nutrients and life necessary to develop us into "mature Christians." We will learn more about becoming a "mature Christian" in the chapter, "Attaining the Character of Christ."

The Teakettle Experience

Prophet Jeremiah had a "teakettle experience." He exclaimed that the Word was in his heart as a burning fire shut up in his bones (Jer. 20:9). A teakettle comes to mind when I read that scripture. The water inside of a teakettle reaches a boiling point whenever heat or fire is applied. The boiling pressure causes the teakettle to whistle and to vent steam. Prophet Jeremiah was saying in this particular scripture that if he were not allowed to speak about the Lord, about the Word, then the pressure to hold the Word would build up inside of him. The living Word would be a burning fire.

I am reminded of the nursery rhyme about the little teapot that says, "I'm a little teapot short and stout, here is my handle, and here is my spout. When I get all steamed up you hear me shout, just tip me over, and pour me out." Why not become a little teapot for Jesus? Fill ourselves up with the Word and allow it to brew inside of us through the meditation of our heart. Whenever we meditate or study the Word, it becomes rich and strong like tea that is brewed for a long period. The Word can richly bless our lives and others.

Our personal teakettle experience occurs whenever we gain more insight or understanding of a particular scripture. The "water of the Word" begins to boil on the inside of us. The Word ignites a continuous burning flame in our heart, which then creates a desire within us to tell someone what we have learned. We become "steamed

Whenever we meditate or study the Word, it becomes rich and strong like tea that is brewed for a long period.

up" and begin to shout it out! It is difficult to remain silent when the inward fire for the Word increases. Then the hand of God will position us to bless others with the words of our mouth. The Word will just flow out of us so that others can drink of His goodness.

Look what happened to the disciples when they spent quality time with Jesus and with the scriptures. They had a teakettle experience too. Luke 24:32 says, *They said one to another, did not our heart burn within us, while He talked with us by the way, and while He opened to us the scriptures?* This verse tells us how to ignite a fire to burn deep within on the altars of our heart. The disciples talked to Jesus and He talked to them. Jesus openly shared and revealed scriptures to them during their times together.

We, too, need to set aside quality time to communicate with God through our prayers, and through praise and worship. As we read, study, and meditate on the scriptures, the Holy Spirit enlightens our understanding and gives us the ability to apply the Word to our life. Our hearts will burn with passion for God even more when we increase our time in the Word.

The entire chapter of Psalm 119 should be called a word about the Word because the psalmist covers what the Word will do for us and how we are to respond to it.

Psalm 119 — The Word

- Teaches righteousness (vss. 7, 75, 106, 137)
- Directs our path (vs. 133)
- Keeps our way pure (vs. 9)
- Gives us the commandments of God (vs. 172)
- Keeps us from sin (vs. 10)
- Quickens us (vss. 25, 50)
- Strengthens us (vs. 28)
- Keeps us until the end (vs. 33)
- Gives us liberty and freedom (vs. 45)
- Gives us hope (vss. 49, 74, 82, 114)
- Comforts us (vss. 50, 76)
- Teaches us good judgment and knowledge (vs. 66)
- Gives us sound reasoning (vs. 80)
- Is the final authority and is settled in heaven (vs. 89)
- Gives light and understanding (vss. 99, 133)

- Is sweet and tasty to our spirit (vs. 103)
- Is a lamp to our feet and a light to our path (vs. 105)
- Is the righteousness of God (vs. 123)
- Is pure and true (vss. 140, 160)
- Gives us peace (vs. 165)

Psalm 119 — We Should

- Love the Word (vss. 47, 48, 97)
- Live in the Word (vs. 17)
- Keep the Word (vss. 17, 55-58)
- Hide the Word in our hearts (vs. 10)
- Meditate in the Word and on the Ways of God (vss. 15, 23, 48, 78, 97, 99, 148)
- Delight ourselves in the Word (vss. 16, 47, 77, 174)
- Behold the things in the Word (vs. 18)
- Talk about His wondrous works (from the Word and in our lives) (vs. 27)
- Observe the Word with our whole heart (vs. 34)
- Seek God and His precepts in the Word (vs. 45)
- Believe the Word (vs. 66)
- Learn the ways of God by learning the Word (vss. 71, 73)
- Rejoice in our hearts over the Word (vss. 111, 162)
- Purpose in our hearts to obey the Word (vs. 112)
- Stand in awe of the Word (vs. 161)
- Speak the Word (vs. 172)

**We can always refer back to
Psalm 119
whenever we need
a reminder of why we need the Word.**

The Soil — The Heart

God's Word is a seed waiting to be planted inside our hearts. Jesus shared a parable about four types of people and how they received the Word of God. In the first case, the person only hears the Word. The seed is on the surface and not rooted, therefore, the devil comes along and takes the seed. In the second case, the person hears the Word and receives the Word with great joy. The seed is planted, but has no root. This person is not well grounded in the Word and during times of temptation, he falls. It's almost like the seed was never planted. In the next case, the person hears the Word, goes forth in the Word, but is consumed with the thorny cares, riches, and pleasures of this life. This person is so consumed that the seed never develops into fruit. In the last case, the seed is planted in good ground or good soil, and the person hears the Word, keeps the Word in his heart, and with patience brings forth good fruit. You see in the first three cases, the seed never had the opportunity to grow. The seed was present only for a short period before it was destroyed. In order for spiritual growth to occur, the seed must remain intact. We all desire to be that person who brings forth good fruit, but our first challenge is to have the Word (seed) of God planted and rooted in our hearts. As we go forth, we are to apply the Word to our daily lives. Then we are to patiently wait for the seed to grow in our hearts in order to bring forth good fruit in due season.

2 Timothy 3:16-17 tells us that *"all scripture was given by inspiration of God, and is profitable for doctrine, for reproof, for correction, for instruction in righteousness: that the man of God may be perfect, thoroughly furnished unto all good works."* We can call the Bible our instruction book, road map, blueprint, game plan, or rulebook. Choose whichever term fits your style because they all allude to the same message; the scriptures were written to help us. The scriptures were written to be a guide for us and to keep us on the righteous path. They were written so that we might become like Jesus. Whenever we read the Bible, many times the Holy Spirit will convict our hearts if we have been walking in disobedience to the Word. God knows how to correct us in a gentle but firm way. Whenever we are not certain of what to do, we should always use the Word of God as the measuring stick for truth.

The Word is sharper than any two edged sword. We are to hold up the Word in our defense against satan, while shielding ourselves with faith to quench every fiery dart that the enemy throws our way. The Word is so intertwined with faith that we cannot separate them.

Helpful Hint

Become a student of God's Word. Begin to search the scriptures so

that the Holy Spirit can enlighten your understanding. Read the book

of Proverbs to learn of God's wisdom. Breathe life into others by

speaking the Word of God over their lives. Spend time in the Word,

in prayer, and in praise and worship as often as you can.

3: The Chambers of God
The Passageway of Faith

We always thank God, the Father of our Lord Jesus Christ, when we pray for you, because we have heard of your faith in Christ Jesus and of the love you have for all the saints—the faith and love that spring from the hope that is stored up for you in heaven and that you have already heard about in the word of truth, the gospel that has come to you.

All over the world this gospel is bearing fruit and growing, just as it has been doing among you since the day you heard it and understood God's grace in all its truth. — Colossians 1:3-6

Faith goes wherever the *living water* flows. We learned that the *living water* is the Word of truth. According to Romans 10:17, faith comes by hearing the Word of God. Colossians 1:3-6 tells us that faith springs from that which we have heard from the Word of truth. Each of us has been given a measure of faith from God (Rom. 12:3). That faith is described by Jesus as a mustard seed, meaning it starts small but has the potential to grow into a great tree. By faith, we accepted Jesus Christ as Lord, and it will take faith to effectively grow that relationship. However, what is faith? Faith is the substance of things hoped for and the evidence of things not seen (Heb. 11:1). The Word of God gives us hope, and the substance of our hope is faith. If you can imagine, think of our faith as being a muscle that we are to exercise on a daily basis. Muscles are to be exercised or else they become weak, cramped, extremely tight, or shortened. Faith comes by hearing the Word of God. We are to exercise our faith in believing God's Word. In believing for the promises of God to manifest within our lives, our faith will grow and become strong. God allows customized situations to occur in order for each of us to stretch our muscle of faith. Our faith is then no longer weak, but made stronger if we faint not and continue to have faith through those situations.

Our victory depends on our mental disposition. Having an attitude of faith will lead us to victory. Whenever satan throws thoughts that are contrary to the Word, we are to shield ourselves with faith to quench every fiery dart.

It is by grace and through faith that we are saved (Eph. 2: 8). The righteous are to live by faith (Gal. 3:11). The righteous are justified by faith (Gal. 3:24). Faith is one of the fruit of the Spirit (Gal. 5:22). Through faith in Jesus, we approach God (Eph. 3:12). The shield of faith is part of our spiritual armor (Eph. 6:16). By faith, God formed the universe (Heb. 11:3). Without faith, it is impossible to please God (Heb. 11:6). Like our forefathers listed in Hebrews 11, we can become more than conquerors through our faith.

Faith is what plugs us into God. Faith operates like the end of a power cord and releases authority. Putting our faith in the wrong things can be very destructive. There is an old movie that gives us a good example of this. In this movie there was an old scary man with steel razor hands. Many of the characters within the movie were afraid of him and believed that he had the power to come into their dreams and harm them. This old man had power and authority over them because of their beliefs. Once they realized that they didn't have to believe in him, they began to say, "I take back the power that I have given you, I don't believe in you anymore." The old man could no longer come into their dreams. Jesus Christ is the only one that we can trust to give that kind of authority and power over our lives. God will lead us through difficult processes, but He will not bring us harm. God has good thoughts towards us. We must put our faith in God. Give Him the power and authority to perform miracles in our lives. When we put our faith in God, we give Him the authority, power, and permission to intervene in any and all areas of our life. *"And we know that in all things God works for the good of those who love him, who have been called according to his purpose"* (Rom. 8:28).

We are justified by faith, but faith without works is dead (James 2:24-26). Our faith must be active to be effective. In other words, it takes our faith and our actions working together to make our faith complete. Abraham is an example of active faith in the Bible.

Was not our ancestor Abraham considered righteous for what he did when he offered his son Isaac on the altar? You see that his faith and his actions were working together, and his faith was made complete by what he did.

— James 2:21-22

If you were to do a search on the words "by faith," you would find that in most cases an action word is associated with it.

"By Faith"

- Sanctified by faith
- Circumcised of the heart by faith
- Live by faith
- Justified by faith
- Stand by faith
- Walk by faith
- Wait by faith (actively wait)
- And everything that does not come by faith is sin (Rom. 14:23)

When we have faith in God, His grace gives us the strength to walk out the *will* of God. Walking out the will of God is not always easy, but God rewards the faithful. Ezekiel had visions that are filled with symbolism relating to the temple of God. We can create an analogy with his vision in regards to our walk of faith with God. We will now take a walk through the vision described in Ezekiel 40 and 41. Throughout these chapters, we are given little nuggets to apply to our lives.

The first thing Ezekiel saw in the vision was God taking him to the land of Israel and he sat at a high place. Then Ezekiel saw a man standing by a building or house with several measuring devices in his hands.

The man then spoke to him saying, "watch and listen and take to heart everything I show you, for you have been brought here so I can show you many things; and then you are to return to the people to tell them all you have seen" (Ezek. 40:4).

The man in the vision began to measure the wall around this building. We will call this building the Temple.

They approached a gate, which was facing the east, a door, and an opening. They entered into the hall of the passage. Within this hall, there were several little chambers. The man measured the outside of every little chamber or small room. Each chamber had a window that narrowed inward, going from a large opening on the outside to a narrow opening inside. Palm trees were upon each post. The palm trees are symbols of victory.

The man continued to take Ezekiel forth until they reached the outer court of the Temple. They had been walking all of this time through a long hall with many little rooms along the way. Each room had a narrow window with a palm tree located on a post outside of the room. When they were in the outer court, they saw more gates and passageways containing more chambers, this time on pavement like hot stone or coal. There were also posts, arches, and palm trees.

The post represents anything that is strong in nature such as a mighty man, an oak, ram, or tree. The arches were the openings of pillars or standing columns. Everything within this vision is symbolic for us. The long passageways are like our life journeys. They are the pathways for our walks of faith. As we proceed on our faith journeys, the process often seems so long. It sometimes seems like it will take forever for change to come. It may seem like forever before that goal is achieved, but we must trust God to direct us and keep us until we have the victory.

We see each other passing by and we smile or wave, and say, "hey, how are you doing today? I'm doing all right or just fine thank you." We can see that we're all progressing on our journeys. What happens, however, when God decides to take each of us into one of those little chambers where the windows are so narrow? Within that little chamber, we feel all alone and it seems so dark on the inside. There is only one little narrow window. Our vision becomes narrowed and the windows of our faith are really slim at this point. Faith is how we as Christians are suppose to see, for we are to walk by faith and not by sight. The chambers are those situations that we walk into throughout our lives that cause us to feel like we are all alone. It makes us feel as if we are isolated and no one else is going through anything. Our outlook on life in that situation we are experiencing begins to appear really dark (losing hope), and our faith begins to decrease. Our faith begins to narrow. We begin to question our obedience to God, saying, "Why should I keep doing this if things are not going well for me. All my efforts are failing. I don't understand what is happening God. I am walking in obedience, as far as I know, why am I in this situation, this little chamber?"

God wants us to be encouraged. He is working something in us during those periods when He brings us into our personal chamber. These little chambers are like waiting rooms. It's those circumstances in our lives that put us in a waiting period. We wait for God to move the obstacles. We wait for God to move on our behalf. We wait on God to bring about achievement in our goals and bring us to victory. Patience is acquired in those waiting rooms chambers. God makes us wait on many things so that we may grow in patience. God is always into character building.

Now, if faith without works is dead, what are we to do with our faith while we are waiting in a chamber? The post, the arches, and palm trees were all outside the chambers. Which means, when we are in a season of waiting, we need to look outside of our situation and by faith see the post, by faith see the arches, and by faith see the palm trees. By faith, we need to see the post to remind us that God is strengthening us in the process and that He will give us a backbone of steel to withstand the trials that we experience in life. We also need to see the arches to remind us that we are not alone. The arches remind us that God is with us and will be our support every step of the way. The arches also signify how we should stand firm in the midst of a spiritual storm or to show that as we are going through, we can stand and be a support system for others who are going through their personal challenges. We can be an encouragement for someone else. By faith, we can see the leaves waving on the palm tree shouting, "victory is near, victory is here! We have the victory in the name of Jesus!"

Now we are ready for the inner court. The inner court was designed pretty much like the outer court in that it contained gates, chambers, post, arches, and palm trees. The interesting details about the inner court in this vision are that there were several series of steps. There was one set of seven steps and two sets of eight steps. In the inner court we must step beyond our past hurts and disappointments, and embrace second chances and new beginnings.

In the inner court, there was also a special chamber for the singers. How neat is that? The praisers and worshipers had a special place in the inner court. There were two other chambers in the inner court. One chamber was for the priest who helped to maintain the house of God. The second chamber was for the priest who ministered and kept the altar. Our chamber experiences will be determined by the call on our lives or our placement within the body of Christ.

The man in the vision then led Ezekiel further into the inner court, which was like the Most Holy Place. The chambers in the inner court all wound upward. In this place, God takes us from our lowest to the highest point as we put our faith in Him and trust Him to guide us. There were wide areas or large spaces between each chamber in the Most Holy Place, which implies that it will take us more time to advance from one chamber to the next. Another interesting place was the area called the separate place (temple courtyard). Whenever necessary, the hand of God will guide us to that separate place. He literally begins to separate us from others who may hinder His will for our lives. Sometimes those seasons of separation can be painful, especially if we begin to feel as if we are missing out on something. Sometimes God will separate us from others or things when we become too attached and dependent. We are drawn closer to God while in this separate place. Another good point about being in this separate place is that we are set apart for God to do a work within us.

Lastly are the galleries and cherubim. The galleries are like a ledge on a building. Have you ever felt like you were on a ledge? In the galleries, we cannot see out of the windows because they are covered. We really have to depend on God for guidance, totally walking by faith and believing His promises to manifest without any physical reminders of the promise. The Cherubim were between the palm trees at this level. The angels of God are present to help us with our victories. Each cherub had two faces, one may symbolize our victories when we face man, while the other might represent our victories when we face those roaring situations.

In summary, Ezekiel's vision represents our faith walk with God. We should be constant, continuing to progress forward no matter what we are faced with along the passageway. Our faith is to increase as we advance to new levels in God. We are to walk by faith and not by sight knowing that God will not leave us in a dark place, but will move us forward as we continue with Him. In that progression, we will see victory, receive strength, stand firm, and extol praise to our Lord.

In Ezekiel 43:2-5, the glory of God fills the house. Behold, God is taking us into these chambers, taking us higher in Him so that we can see His glory. In God's appointed time, we will experience His glory operating in us and through us greatly, as we trust Him to take us from chamber to chamber.

> Our light and momentary troubles are achieving for us an eternal glory that far outweighs them all. So we fix our eyes not on what is seen, but on what is unseen, for what is seen is temporary, but what is unseen is eternal.
> — 2 Corinthians 4:17-18

Our prayer life usually increases during those waiting periods and seasons of preparation. We learn how to intercede, we learn how to travail, and we learn to cry out to God. We learn to seek His face in those secret places.

4. Secret Hiding Place
Prayer as a Place of Refuge

He that dwells in the secret place of the Most High shall abide under the shadow of the Almighty. — Psalm 91:1 As the deer pants for streams of water, so my soul pants for you, O God. My soul thirsts for God, for the living God. When can I go and meet with God? — Psalm 42:1-2

> ## *Pause for Prayer*
>
> *Oh, how I run to my secret hiding place to be alone with my Lord. My soul is thirsty and pants after Thee. I am in need of Your refreshing touch for my spirit is weary; revive me oh God. I need the time alone with You, so that I can rest my mind from mental stress and rest my body from the busyness of the day. I release the demands of the family, of work, of ministry, and of life itself, to You. Oh, how the God of GRACE receives me. And through Your Spirit, the loving arms of Jesus embrace me and bring me peace. Thank you Lord for being my place of refuge, where I can find peace."*

Where do you go when you feel overwhelmed? To whom do you turn for relief? I run to a secret hiding place. For me, a secret hiding place is a place to retreat to be alone with the Lord. Creating a secret hiding place for yourself and the Lord is necessary in order to remain refreshed, with a faith attitude and a heart of gratitude. Once you have met the Lord with some frequency in a particular place to spend time with Him, your spirit will begin to automatically respond to Him as soon as you enter that place. Sometimes you are not even conscience of your thoughts or actions. It is as if you are on autopilot.

Over the years, I have discovered several secret places to meet the Lord. My car has become a secret hiding place during my one-hour commute to work. As soon as I settle in, without even thinking, I begin to talk to God or I begin to sing to Him. Many times, I will take my lunch break at the company park just to be alone with my Lord for moments of silence and peace. The shower is another place of retreat for me. I have three little ones and interruptions at home are less likely to occur when I am in this place. Again, like autopilot, as soon as I step in under the flowing water, my spirit responds through speech or song. If I had to choose a favorite spot, it would be a special room located on the second level of our home. Several friends have named it the "upper room" because of the prayer times that we experienced there. My family and I refer to this room as the "work room." The family as a unit often gathers in this room since it serves many functions, such as sewing room, arts and crafts room, computer room, video room, prayer room, worship room, and study room. Whenever I enter alone, I can sense God's presence as if He were waiting for me. This is the room where I spent hours writing this book. Quality time in studying God's Word is spent there; revelation and insight into the scriptures unfolds there. New ideas, dreams, and visions originate right there in that secret hiding place. Some of my most favorable memories with the Lord were spent in that special hiding place. My burdens become smaller as God is magnified through my prayers, singing, and dance before Him. Regardless of which secret place I am in, God will drop little golden nuggets in my spirit.

If you have not yet created a secret hiding place, wait no longer. What better time than now. As I stated earlier, the frequency of meeting the Lord in a certain place will cause your time with Him to become spontaneous and unrehearsed. Your times will become electrifying as you begin to automatically respond to the Lord. Your spirit will become more sensitive to the Lord, and with anticipation, you will wait for the next retreat.

Pray the Word

Prayer is another spiritual element that is essential to our spiritual growth. It is foundational for every strong, anointed ministry. Prayer takes us into a deeper relationship with God. Ministries experience much opposition; therefore, all leaders must especially know how to wage effective warfare against the enemy. Effective warfare is accomplished through the Word in prayer (and praise). The Word of God is the sword of the Spirit. We are to clothe ourselves with the proper armor on a daily basis so that we might stand when opposition comes. We must take up our sword and learn how to apply it within our prayers. Hebrews 4:12 declares, *"The word of God is living, active, and sharper than any double-edged sword. It penetrates even to dividing soul and spirit, joints and marrow; it judges the thoughts and attitudes of the heart."* We activate the Word of God to respond on our behalf as we speak it forth. Praying the Word of God is essential in achieving desired results.

There are no greater words more powerful than those written within the scriptures. The Word of God is the Will of God. As we learn to pray the Word of God, we are guided into the Will of God. In order to pray the Word, we must either memorize scriptures or use other available resources to assist us. Several books have been written with scripture prayers that target many specific concerns. These written prayers can be used as a tool. They usually list the referenced scriptures. Written prayers are good as a jumpstart, but from the written prayer we can add words straight from our heart to personalize it or to complete the prayer. Next is an example of a prayer comprised with scriptures.

Our Lord's Prayer

Jesus gave us an outline of how we should pray. The Lord's Prayer in Matthew 6:9-13 covers all of the elements that should be included within our prayers. In this prayer, Jesus teaches that we should pray to the Father in heaven as He prayed while on earth. He then tells us to praise the name of God. Hallowed be thy name signifies to us that God's name is holy, set apart, and should be greatly respected. Within the scriptures we find that many of the attributes of God are defined in names of man and in places that were marked by a name that declares God's faithfulness. It is in those declarations that we find the names of God. The names of God all declare His faithfulness in carrying out promises to every believer. An example of this is given in Jeremiah 33:16, which states, *"In those days Judah will be saved and Jerusalem will live in safety. This is the name by which it will be called: The LORD Our Righteousness."*

Jehovah-Tsidkenu is the name of God that declares the Lord is our Righteousness. We are identified and accepted by the Father because we inherited the righteousness of our Lord; wherein we were adopted as sons into the Family of God, giving us the right to approach Him as Father. Our Heavenly Father accepts and hears the prayers of His sons and daughters. The name Jehovah is found in the root description of many of the Biblical names of man. Jehovah is a name of God. When we pray, we should give thanks and praise to God by calling out the attributes of His character that define Him in all of His sovereignty. Some of those names and attributes are as follows:

Hebrew Names of God

- Elohim: Supreme and only true God, the Creator (Gen. 1:1)
- El Shaddai: God Almighty (Exod. 6:3)
- Jehovah Jireh: The Lord will Provide (Gen. 22:14)
- Jehovah Nissi: The Lord my Banner (Exod. 17:15)
- Jehovah Sabaoth: The Lord God of Hosts (1 Sam. 1:3)
- Jehovah Shammah: The Lord is There (Ezek. 48:35)
- Jehovah Shalom: The Lord is Peace (Judg. 6:24)
- Jehovah Yahweh: I Am Who I Am (Exod. 3:14)

After giving thanks and praise, we are instructed to pray, *"Thy Kingdom come. Thy will be done on earth as it is in heaven."* We are asking God to manifest His righteousness, peace, and joy in our hearts. We are asking Him to perform His Will in our lives. When the *will* that resides within our heart becomes submitted to the Word of God, we experience righteousness, peace, and joy in the Holy Ghost.

For the kingdom of God is not meat and drink; but righteousness, and peace, and joy in the Holy Ghost.

— Romans 14:17

Pause for Prayer (Colossians 1:9-14)

Heavenly Father, I pray that You will fill me with the knowledge of Your will in all wisdom and spiritual understanding. I pray that You help me live a life worthy of the Lord so that I may please You in every way, bearing fruit in every good work, and growing in the knowledge of You more and more each day. I pray that You strengthen me with all might according to Your glorious power, so that I might joyfully have great endurance and patience. I give thanks to You Father. You have qualified me to share in the inheritance of the saints in the kingdom of light. You have rescued me from the dominion of darkness and brought me into the kingdom of Your Son, Jesus Christ, in whom I have redemption and forgiveness of my sins. Thank You Jesus for saving me by Your blood. Thank You Father for accepting me as a son. In the name of Jesus, I pray. Amen.

We pray for the will of the Father as Jesus prayed. Following that request, we can ask God for His provision. We ask Him to make provision for our daily needs. It doesn't matter if our needs are physical, emotional, or spiritual. We should not feel guilty in making those requests.

Our Lord's Prayer reveals His forgiving nature. We must forgive others for words or actions that make us feel violated or offended. The Father will forgive us of our trespasses as we forgive others that trespass against us.

"Lead us not into temptation, but deliver us from evil," is a request that we should make often. We are acknowledging God in our prayer, asking that His Spirit direct our path. We are asking that He lead us in ways that are void of temptations, and when those evil enticements do come, we are asking that He deliver us out of the situation.

Our prayers are to begin with thanksgiving and praise and should end with more praise. Again, we declare His kingdom, His power, and His glory with our praise. Since Jesus is the only way to the Father in heaven, we must pray in the Name of Jesus. Since we have a relationship with God, just our average conversation to Him is counted as prayer. Prayer is our way of verbally communicating with God.

Pray in the Spirit

The Holy Spirit was given to us as a gift. Jesus sent His Spirit to abide with us after He ascended into Heaven to the right hand of the Father. The Spirit enables us to pray in other tongues. We should not be afraid of tongues for it is a heavenly language given to believers. As believers in Christ, we can activate our spiritual language by allowing the Spirit to pray through us. Speaking with new tongues is one of the signs that Jesus promised would follow every believer (Mark 16: 17). It is a language that is foreign to our natural minds. Whenever we pray in tongues, the Holy Spirit prays to God through us. The Spirit is making intercession for us according to the will of God for our lives. Many times when we go to God in prayer, we don't always know where to start, or what to pray, but the Spirit is never at a loss for words.

Our spiritual language is a weapon against the enemy because it confuses him and he knows not what we are speaking. Even though satan is the prince of the air, he has no power to intercept our prayers when prayed in the spirit (1 Cor. 14:2). Ephesians 6:18 encourages us to pray in the spirit on all occasions.

> And pray in the Spirit on all occasions with all kinds of prayers and requests. With this in mind, be alert and always keep on praying for all the saints. — Ephesians 6:18

I have often used tongues as my defense against the enemy. I would use my spiritual language to intercept any thought within my mind that was contrary to the Word of God. By praying in the spirit, the Holy Spirit would immediately arrest any unhealthy thoughts. After learning to pray in tongues on a daily basis, my spiritual walk became more stable. I was no longer easily shaken by what I thought, heard, or saw. I would just begin to pray in tongues. If something did jolt me, I would soon recover through prayer. We were given our spiritual languages to keep ourselves built up in our most holy faith and to strengthen us spiritually (Jude 20). This scripture links us back to our chapter on *faith*. Rivers of living water flow out of our belly when we pray in the spirit, to build us up in our faith in Jesus. This river will cause our faith to spring forth and increase even more.

> He that believeth on me, as the scripture hath said, out of his belly shall flow rivers of living water. (But this spoke he of the Spirit, which they that believe on him should receive: for the Holy Ghost was not yet given; because that Jesus was not yet glorified.) — John 7:38-39

If you have not yet activated your spiritual language, just ask God to fill you with His Spirit anew. Then begin to pray in your native language while relaxing your language so that the Spirit can take control of your tongue. At first the words of your new tongues may sound like baby talk; but remember, the development of your spiritual language is like a baby because you have never used it. Your tongues will develop into an adult language as you continue to pray in tongues on a daily basis. Over time you may find that your tongues change to another spiritual language as you pray, which means that you have been given the gift of diversities of tongues. Maybe you are unsure on whether or not to activate your spiritual  language. It is your decision; God will not override your personal will. However, the benefit of having an active spiritual language provides another level of intimacy with God.

Our Enemy

An important key to remember is that our battle is not with flesh and blood, but it is spiritual. We fight against principalities, powers, and spiritual wickedness in high places. The enemy can use our own minds as a weapon against us, by dropping in thoughts that are contrary to God's Word, such as negative thoughts, discouraging thoughts, or tormenting thoughts. Moreover, the worst thing a person can do is to believe those contrary thoughts and accept them as their own. We are to pull down every imagination that exalts itself against the knowledge of God. How else will we be able to recognize a thought that is contrary to the Word except we read the Scriptures? We can speak God's Word as a weapon to bring contrary thoughts into captivity. In order to be a victorious Christian, we must bring our "thought lives" into submission to the Word of God.

The enemy will also use religious spirits to bring division, such as the sinful attributes of the flesh. Following are some of the attributes of the flesh that are compared to the attributes of the Spirit, the Fruit of the Spirit. We should pray fort God to guard our heart against those things that are of a sinful nature and pray to reflect the nature of Christ.

> But if you are led by the Spirit, you are not under law. The acts of the sinful nature are obvious: sexual immorality, impurity and debauchery; idolatry and witchcraft; hatred, discord, jealousy, fits of rage, selfish ambition, dissensions, factions and envy; drunkenness, orgies, and the like. I warn you, as I did before, that those who live like this will not inherit the kingdom of God. But the fruit of the Spirit is love, joy, peace, patience, kindness, goodness, faithfulness, gentleness, and self-control. Against such things there is no law. Those who belong to Christ Jesus have crucified the sinful nature with its passions and desires. Since we live by the Spirit, let us keep in step with the Spirit. Let us not become conceited, provoking and envying each other. — Galatians 5:18-26

Pray Against the Spirits of	Pray For the Spirit of
• Pride	• Humility
• Control	• Love
• Conflict/Division	• Unity

- Rebellion
- Fear
- Competition
- Despair
- Anxiety
- Jealousy and Envy
- Intimidation

- Obedience
- Faith
- Cooperation
- Joy
- Peace
- Thankfulness
- Holy Boldness (Confidence in God)

Jesus provided the model prayer to help guide in our prayers. His prayer provided all of the elements that produce an effective prayer. These elements are not meant to become a religious ritual, but rather to enhance our time with God. The most important thing to remember is God desires relationship with us, not a religious prayer with vain repetitions. We are to pray from our hearts. Our prayer life is an extension of our relationship with Christ. Out of that relationship, we talk to Him on a regular basis. We share our heart and He shares His. We wake up talking to Him and throughout the day, we ask for guidance and instructions.

Keys Elements to an Effective Prayer[2]

- **Thanksgiving and Praise**
  According to Philippians 4:6, we are to incorporate words of thanksgiving within our prayers and petitions. The Word encourages us to approach God with a heart of gratitude and to enter His courts with praise.

- **Supplication**
  Supplication is asking and making your request known to God. Supplication can be done by the spirit through praying in tongues, or in your natural language (words of understanding).

- **Confession and Repentance**
  We are under grace, because of the blood of Jesus, but we still need to confess our sins, repent, and ask for forgiveness. Live repentant lives before the Father, making certain that all of our actions, conscious and unconscious, are covered under the blood of Jesus.

- **Scriptures**
  Pray the scriptures concerning our request. Pray the promises of God, speaking those promises that He has made to you back to Him.

- **Worship and Adoration**
  Worship Him for who He is and for being All Mighty.

One may ask, in what order should we pray or how should we come before the Lord in prayer. We can always follow the model that Jesus gave us. As stated earlier, we are to enter into God's presence with thanksgiving and praise. Having a repentant heart is never a bad way to start. Also, we can't go wrong when we pray in the Spirit and pray the Word. The Word is our lifeline. As we allow both the Word and prayer to flow consistently in and through our hearts, relationship and intimacy with the Lord develops. In the next chapter, we will go back to the beginning, to that moment of rebirth, where we first met Jesus and then progress to intimacy.

Pause for Prayer: "The Dancer's Prayer"

Dear Father, As I come to offer my gift of praise unto You, I cast every care and burden upon You. I ask that You forgive me of anything that I have done in word or deed that was not pleasing to You. I thank You for the redeeming blood of Jesus, my Savior. I thank You for the depths of Your Mercy and the abundance of Your Grace. Help me to walk in love and be reconciled with anyone whom I have offended so that my offering of praise will be acceptable unto You. I enter Your gates with Thanksgiving and Your courts with Praise. I give thanks to You and Praise Your name. Search me and know my heart. Lead me into Your everlasting way. Help me to worship You in spirit and in truth in all that I do. Allow my life to be a light to others and worship unto You. I give praise to You oh God, for the Joy of the Lord is my strength. You are the reason that I Dance! In Jesus Name. Amen.

Helpful Hint

During your personal prayer times, it's a good idea to keep a notebook and pen to capture the words or thoughts that God drops in your spirit. Keep praise or worship music in your secret hiding place to play as desired.

5: Relationship With Christ
Developing an Intimate Connection with God

In the beginning, the most creative account in history was made when God decided, 'let Us make man.' God created the heavens and the earth and everything within them. He created man and woman in His own image. Adam and Eve were the first man and woman to dwell in God's holy presence. God's presence was felt as He walked among them in the Garden of Eden.

He was all they knew outside of each other and the wild life surrounding them.

When sin came into the picture, the divine presence departed from Adam and Eve and they were banished from the Garden. God placed two cherubim and a flaming sword at the east of the garden, to guard the way to the Tree of Life. Adam and Eve experienced a great deprivation once they lost the most vital part of their lives. They lost the free access they once had to the presence of God. A deep void longing to be filled formed within them. When Adam and Eve sinned against God, their connection with God was severed. Their spiritual umbilical cord was cut by sin and they became separated from that holy fellowship. This separation was never intended.

We naturally have a desire for relationship, to belong, and to connect with someone. God likewise has a desire for relationship with us. That original holy connection disintegrated with the fall of the first Adam. Since sin now separates mankind from God, there is a void that cannot be filled except by God. In attempting to fill that void, a person will search for fulfillment in all the wrong places never finding true joy, true peace, or true love. Jesus Christ, the second

Adam came to redeem us back to Himself so that we might have a Garden of Eden experience with Him. Jesus Christ came to redeem and restore that divine connection. He came so that we might have a connection of oneness with God the Father again. He came that we might have a connection with holiness, a connection with true love, a connection with grace, a connection with mercy, a connection with compassion, a connection with true joy, and a connection with true abundant life and eternal life.

John 3:3 tells us that we must be born again in order to be able to see the kingdom of God. In other words, we must experience a spiritual birthing. We must experience a supernatural reconnection with God before we can experience His fullness, and the manifestation of His kingdom glory and principles operating within our lives. As stated in 1 Peter 1:23, we must be born again of incorruptible seed, by the Word of God.

When a baby is inside of the mother's womb there is an intimate connection between mother and child. Fellowship between the mother and child will transpire throughout the gestation period. Whatever the mother eats, the baby will eat also. Whatever the mother drinks, the baby will drink. Whatever the mother does can and will affect the baby. That is why expectant mothers are asked to watch their diet. The connection between mother and child is made through the umbilical cord. The umbilical cord is the necessary link for blood flow, the link that propagates growth. Without the umbilical cord, there is no life for the baby.

A baby is birthed through the birth canal, and passes from one environment to another. The baby can no longer function in this new environment as in the former. In entering this new environment, the old ways of living pass away and all things become new to that newborn baby. The doctor clears out the air passageway with a suction device. The baby then takes his first breath and the lungs begin to function. It's a whole new world! This baby experiences life in a new way. The birthing experience is a powerful demonstration of the awesomeness of God giving life to His creation. The next thing that takes place after that first breath of life is the cutting of the umbilical cord. The baby becomes physically disconnected from the mother. The baby then receives forms of nutrition through the breast or bottle. As the child grows, the diet is modified accordingly. The development process continues through adulthood.

My intent in sharing this example about the natural birthing of a baby is to compare that experience to the spiritual birthing of a newborn in Christ. Jesus told Nicodemus that a man must be born again. Nicodemus then asked, *"How can a man be born when he is old? Can he enter the second time into his mother's womb, and be born?"* Nicodemus did not understand that Jesus was speaking of a spiritual birth. Jesus answered, *"Verily, verily, I say unto thee, except a man must be born of water and of the Spirit he cannot enter into the Kingdom of God. That which is born of the flesh is flesh; and that which is born of the Spirit is spirit"* (John 3:4-6). To be born of the Spirit, we must ask Jesus Christ to come into our heart to become our personal Lord and Savior. At that very moment, the regeneration process begins to take place in our lives and the spiritual birth occurs.

> For we ourselves also were sometimes foolish, disobedient, deceived, serving divers lusts and pleasures, living in malice and envy, hateful, and hating one another. But after that the kindness and love of God our Saviour toward man appeared, not by works of righteousness which we have done, but according to his mercy he saved us, by the washing of regeneration, and renewing of the Holy Ghost; which he shed on us abundantly through Jesus Christ our Saviour; That being justified by his grace, we should be made heirs according to the hope of eternal life. — Titus 3:3-7

During the regeneration process, the Spirit of Jesus, the Holy Spirit becomes a part of us, who at the same time is a part of the Father. Jesus came to restore that spiritual connection with God the Father. He came to reconnect the spiritual umbilical cord that gives us spiritual life. Jesus is our spiritual umbilical cord. He is the *biblical cord*. Without Jesus, there is no way to the Father. Jesus said it Himself in John 14:6, "I am the way, the truth, and the life: no man cometh unto the Father, but by me."

Now that we understand that a spiritual birthing must take place in order for the spiritual umbilical cord to be reconnected to God, are you sure that you know Jesus as your personal Lord and

Savior? You may recite the prayer below to establish or reestablish that relationship. Jesus came that we may have life and life more abundantly.

Pause for Prayer

Dear Heavenly Father, I thank You for sending Your Son Jesus to die on the cross for me to be saved. I believe that Jesus died, was resurrected, and ascended into heaven and is now seated on the throne of God at Your right hand. Please forgive me of all of my sin. Jesus I ask You now to come into my heart and save me. Please save me from my past and from an unexpected end. I ask that You fill me with Your Holy Spirit so that I might have a helper to keep me in this new way of living. I thank You for sending Your Spirit to comfort me and to teach me of Your way. In the Name of Jesus I pray. Amen.[1]

For God so loved the world, that he gave his only begotten Son, that whosoever believeth in him should not perish, but have everlasting life. For God sent not his Son into the world to condemn the world; but that the world through him might be saved. — John 3:16-17

That if you confess with your mouth, "Jesus is Lord," and believe in your heart that God raised him from the dead, you will be saved. For it is with your heart that you believe and are justified, and it is with your mouth that you confess and are saved. — Romans 10:9-10

If you prayed the prayer of faith above or if you have made that confession in the past, you are now grafted into the body of believers, the body of Christ. A birthing of a higher degree has taken place. The spiritual umbilical cord is re-connected from God to man.

Webster defines the umbilical cord to be more than just a cordlike structure that connects the child to the mother. An umbilical cord is also the cable connecting an astronaut to his or her ship while out in space. It is a power supply line to a rocket or spacecraft preceding take off.[2] This definition is so relative to our relationship with Jesus. In my personal definition, it is the power cord linking the saints to Father God. Jesus is that cable or cord that connects us to the Father, and our faith plugs us in. We are in this world, but not of this world, so we need a cord to keep us anchored in the Word. Jesus is the power supply line that allows us to receive strength and ability from God the Father to reach the heights that He has purposed for us to achieve.

Pause for Prayer: The Anchor Prayer

Dear Lord, You are my source of life. You are my source for strength. My soul is anchored in You. Please help me to stay in the Word and to obey Your Word. Thank you for making me one with God the Father. Thank you for sending Your Holy Spirit to lead me, giving me full assurance of eternal life that has been promised.

Unlike the natural birthing process, it is essential that the spiritual umbilical cord remain connected to Jesus. If cut, spiritual growth will be halted. The blood of Jesus is our conduit or spiritual umbilical cord that connects us to God the Father. As indicated in "The Pattern for Worship" chapter, the blood was shed as an act of atonement. Atonement is the act by which God restores relationship and fellowship between Himself and mankind. Jesus shed His innocent blood as an act of atonement, giving all the opportunity to become *one* with God the Father again.

Now that the divine connection has been restored, the proper nutrients and spiritual diet must be provided to assist in our spiritual growth. What is the makeup of this spiritual diet and how does one grow spiritually? It is through the Word of God, it is through prayer, and it is through praise. All are essential in our relationship with God.

Developing Intimacy with God

Our relationship with God was designed to go deeper than just being a born again believer. Developing a life style of worship through prayer, praise, and the Word enables us to communicate with God from our hearts. Just as we share our heart with a close friend, we have the opportunity to share our heart with Jesus. Our personal prayer times can be transformed into loving sincere moments of worship. Worship is what produces intimacy with the Lord. We are to delight ourselves in the Lord and our souls are to rejoice in Him.

Worship is what produces intimacy with the Lord.

> As a young man marries a maiden, so will your sons marry you; as a bridegroom rejoices over his bride, so will your God rejoice over you.
> — Isaiah 62:5

Jesus is our Bridegroom and the church is His bride. Jesus rejoices over us as His bride. He loves His bride and wants to be close with her. Where there is a bride and groom, there is also intimacy. Jesus Christ is Spirit, and in Him there is no male or female. Therefore, men should not feel bad about becoming intimate with Christ the Bridegroom, because it is our spirit that connects with Him. Intimacy is something of a personal or private nature. Our hearts become united with the Bridegroom as we love Him during our times of prayer and worship. We express our heartfelt thanks to Him for being the lover of our soul, our righteousness, provider, shelter, healer, deliverer, and friend. As those special times of intimacy are created, we enter into spiritual oneness with God, solidifying that relationship. Why not become uninhibited and transparent before the One we love? The Song of Solomon gives us a perfect picture of the intimate relationship that Jesus Christ so desires to have with His bride, the church.[3] He desires that we seek after Him and to long to be in His presence. During those personal prayer times we wait to hear His voice. Several scriptures referring to the bride and bridegroom speak of the sounds of joy and gladness coming from the voices of the bride and the bridegroom. Our heart leaps with joy when He speaks to us. In His presence there is truly fullness of Joy. I believe that the heart of the Lord jumps for joy when we speak words of adoration to Him.

> The bride belongs to the bridegroom. The friend who attends the bridegroom waits and listens for him, and is full of joy when he hears the bridegroom's voice. That joy is mine, and it is now complete. — John 3:29

Often, during my personal prayer times, I pray, dance, and sing before the Lord. As I enter into that place of worship, I worship Him with words and with my entire body in movement. My hands move, my feet move, my entire body responds. Since this is "our" private time, I allow my body to completely relax and move spontaneously before the Lord. My body bows and bends in worship and adoration. At those times, I'm not concerned about how I look. I'm not concerned about technique and poise. Whether the movements are graceful or not is not an issue when it's just me and my Lord. I just love Him through my worship. We dance together and I dance before Him. I enjoy singing to the Lord, and on occasion new worship songs flow out of my spirit.

If this level of intimacy is new for you, then you may want to start by playing worship songs with words that speak your heart towards God, or with words that proclaim His holiness. Allow the song to speak for you. Begin to worship the Lord with your entire body by raising your hands, kneeling, bowing, or lying down prostrate before Him, You will experience moments of expression and moments of silence. During your time of speaking words of adoration to the Lord, start singing to see if a new song will flow from your spirit. God may place a scripture on your heart to meditate on. Each person's experience may be different, but it all builds toward the same goal of intimacy with the Bridegroom. As you practice spending time with God, you will become more relaxed and open, restraining nothing from Him. You will become more familiar with God, with His ways, and know Him as an intimate friend.

> Oh, for the days when I was in my prime, when God's intimate friendship blessed my house, when the Almighty was still with me and my children were around me, when my path was drenched with cream and the rock poured out for me streams of olive oil. — Job 29:4-6

The above verses say that an intimate friendship with God will bless our household. Out of that intimate relationship, "Rivers of Anointing" will flow from God to us. God will cause our lives to shine and radiate, showing His richness and blessings.

King David developed an intimate friendship with God and was considered a man after God's own heart. David spent quality time in prayer and praise. There were rivers of anointing flowing out of David's life, which are evident when we read his writings. The Psalms are filled with the personal prayers of King David. What can we learn from the life of King David? We can glean from the relationship that he had with God.

> Praise the LORD. Sing to the LORD a new song, his praise in the assembly of the saints. Let Israel rejoice in their Maker; let the people of Zion be glad in their King. Let them praise his name with dancing and make music to him with tambourine and harp. For the LORD takes delight in his people; he crowns the humble with salvation. — Psalm 149:1-4

Gleaning from the Good - The Life of King David

David had a special relationship with God. He relates how God protected him while inside his mother's womb. In Psalm 139:13-18, David declares that God did not make a mistake in making him. He understood that even during the moments of conception, God knew his personality, his imperfections, his physical frailties, and his strengths. David recognized that God's thoughts toward him were good. He knew God would always protect him and defeat his enemies. What can we gain from David's attitude and learn from his life? Through his writings, we see that David had a revelation of God as FATHER. David developed a relationship with God early in life. He knew how to crawl into the bosom of the Father whenever he needed comfort. David was a young shepherd when the Lord told the prophet Samuel to anoint him King of Israel. David grew and his faith was tried and tested throughout many seasons of his life. As we look at his life, it is obvious that David learned to wait on the promises of God. Kingship would not be reached overnight. It is not to say that David never became discouraged through the process of waiting, but he knew how to encourage himself by remembering that his Father God was with him every step of the way. He trusted and believed the word of the Lord.

To know God as an intimate friend should be an ongoing mission for us.

David not only had a revelation of God as Father, but he also had a revelation of God as intimate friend. God even referred to David as His friend. David had plenty of quiet time to talk with God while herding the sheep. He was courageous because of his relationship with his God. This courage enabled him to defeat a bear, a lion, and a giant. He did not run from a battle for he learned to put his confidence in the Lord's strength.

Why did David have to remain in the fields learning the skills of a shepherd when he was already anointed to be king? It was because he was in training, learning to serve. He learned to submit and seek after God for help to find that one lost sheep that he loved so much. God was cultivating David's heart to love. All of these attributes were tested during his season as a servant to King Saul. Saul's leadership became corrupt and he became envious of David. Saul sought after David to destroy him, but David remained loyal to Saul and submitted even to the point of having to dodge darts that were thrown at him. David was humble and understood authority. His submission was tested when he denied the opportunity to destroy Saul. During the most difficult season of his life, God birthed new songs through David that would carry us through the ages.

David learned to worship God through good times and challenging times. Worship was a way of life for King David. As king and priest, he set the standard for worship and did not mind laying down his dignity to worship God before the people. He danced before the Lord in complete abandonment. David was an anointed and gifted artist. As musician, he played skillfully and created instruments for the glory of God. He was a prophetic psalmist and wrote poetry. Through worship, David reverenced God and knew Him as an intimate friend.

David knew how to repent. David's heart became defiled with unclean thoughts about Bathsheba, which ultimately led to adultery and premeditated murder. After such a great fall, you would think that it would be almost impossible to recover and return to the Lord, but God had made an investment in David. God knew David and knew exactly how to reach him. Deep down inside, David still had the heart of a shepherd, but he showed little remorse for his sin until after another prophet sought him to bring a word from God. Nathan the prophet was sent to speak with David. Using a parable he painted a word picture about a little lamb that had been slaughtered. The parable captured David's attention for he still had a love for those little lambs. Nathan then proceeded to tell David that he was the man described in the parable (2 Sam. 12:7). At that very moment, tears filled David's eyes and his heart and spirit became broken. David felt remorseful and admitted his sin. The Prophet Nathan responded with these words, "The Lord also has put away your sin and you shall not die." There was, however, a severe consequence to David's sin, the child that Bathsheba conceived died.

David's heart attitude recovered because his relationship with the Lord went deeper than just knowing about Him. The attitude of our heart and relationship with Christ will ultimately determine the depth of our worship. We should welcome God in keeping our hearts and attitudes in check and balance. It is imperative that we spend time with God through quality time in His Word, time in prayer, and through time in praise and worship.

David used his power and authority to take advantage of Bathsheba and Uriah. The lesson that we glean from David's bad experience is we are not to misuse the anointing that has been entrusted to us. We are carriers of the anointing of the Holy Spirit, and that anointing gives us the power and authority to accomplish purpose. We will discuss this more in the following chapters.

To conclude, we can glean many good things from David's life. The main point I wanted to emphasize is his attitude. David learned to repent and rebound from sin whenever he fell short. We can learn from his mistakes. Those difficult moments drew him closer to God. No matter what happened, he knew that His God would deliver him. We, too, will experience seasons of discouragement and seasons of triumph. We see that it is important to be about the Father's business, tending to the task that we have been assigned. As we wait on our ministry, God will seek us out to anoint us for purpose. Lastly, our relationship with God should be solidified through intimate worship. To know God as an intimate friend should be an ongoing mission for us. That relationship will sustain us through all the seasons of our lives.

The attitude of our heart and relationship with Christ will ultimately determine the depth of our worship.

To know Jesus is equivalent to intimacy in relationship, and from that relationship we worship Him. As I mentioned earlier, worship takes us beyond the surface prayers, beyond the outer court, and exterior experiences. Our desire and goal should be to move beyond that outer court experience of praise and into the inner court experience of worship. We become totally abandoned, uninhibited and transparent, unashamed to show our flaws and weaknesses, believing Him to bring healing through His touch and unfailing love.

The difference of an outer court and inner court experience with God is the same difference as praise and worship. It doesn't require relationship to praise God, but true worship requires relationship.

Jesus desires a relationship with you. Will you meet Him in your secret hiding place? He is waiting. I have written a poem to help summarize our relationship with Jesus Christ.

Relationship is to Know Him

Relationship with Christ is to know Him as a friend,
becoming familiar with His ways.
To know Him is to dedicate your life to serve Him
for the rest of your days.
It is to know Him in the beauty of His holiness and
in the fellowship of His sufferings.
To know Him by His Spirit, as comforter, teacher and guide,
The One sent to be with you, to help you abide.
To know Him is to love Him and to
trust Him with all of your heart,
Knowing that His love for you will never ever part.
To know Him is to seek Him and to
recognize His presence as He enters your space.
You long to be near Him and to hear Him
speak to your heart as if face-to-face.
You speak to Him with passion, waiting for Him to respond.
Believing that He has captured your words,
yes each and every one.
To know Him is to hear Him and to obey,
Knowing within your heart He'll never lead you astray.
As you follow His leading, heeding to every word He says,
your desire is to please Him with every breath and move you make.
To know Him is to stand in the midst of uncertainty,
Comforted that it is He who holds your destiny.
Praise to Him comes easy because your love for Him is so great.
You are determined to give praise to Him no matter what it takes.
Your lifestyle has become worship, in your words and deed.
It is so that you know Him, for He meets your every need.

6: Cultivating The Heart
Attaining the Character of Christ

Everything that we've discussed thus far has been leading up to cultivating the heart of a worshiper. We have learned that the primary stream flowing in our lives should be the Word of God. When coupled with faith, prayer, and praise, relationship is developed. Our praise and worship to God increases in significance as we grow in our relationship with Him.

All of these things work together in helping us become true worshipers. As we proceed through this chapter we must keep our minds open so that our hearts may receive what the Spirit of the Lord is saying about "worship" in regards to Godly character. Since the focus is primarily about the heart of the worshiper, mini-breaks may be necessary to give time for reflection.

> Yet a time is coming and has now come when the true worshipers will worship the Father in spirit and truth, for they are the kind of worshipers the Father seeks.
> — John 4:23

God the Father is searching for the true worshipers. We can only become true worshipers over the process of time. The kingdom of God operates in seedtime and harvest. It takes time for the Word seed of God to grow in our hearts. After a period of growth, the fruit that we desire to see will begin to blossom. A wonderful season of harvesting will come and we will enjoy the benefits of new fruit in our lives. We have learned that the seed takes root and grows only when it falls on good soil. This is necessary for us to cultivate our hearts.

Cultivating means to prepare, loosen, or break up the soil, and foster growth. This chapter will prepare our hearts by breaking up the dirt that is inside to help foster spiritual growth in our lives. I will share some personal experiences that will serve as a model to encourage us in our spiritual growth.

The Road to Spiritual Maturity

We must all travel the road to spiritual maturity so that we may acquire the character of Christ. Our experiences, trials, tribulations, and tests of faith are allowed to help develop Godly character. God purposed in His heart for us to know Him and to become like Him.

Our road to spiritual maturity began after we arrived at the major turning point of accepting Jesus Christ as Savior. At that exact moment, regeneration occurred and our sinful nature changed as the Spirit of Jesus entered our hearts. We then had to learn to live according to our new nature.

The natural man is an unsaved individual with a sinful nature, and the carnal minded individual is controlled by the influences of the flesh. A newborn babe of the Spirit has not yet learned or become skilled at applying the elementary truths of the Word to his life. He is vulnerable and may be easily swayed by different doctrines. It is important that newborn babes be taught the attributes pertaining to their new nature, asking the question "What would Jesus do?" Learning and applying the Word to their lives is the challenge that lies ahead.

Our spiritual growth is a process. Through that process our thoughts, attitudes, and actions should change to reflect the nature of Christ. Spoken best by the words of the Apostle Paul in 1 Corinthians 3, our spiritual diets are to grow from milk to meat. The same passage reminds us that carnal mindedness shows a lack of maturity, similar to a newborn babe. We are instructed in Romans to be transformed by the renewing of our minds so that we do not conform to the ways of the world. [1]

God has placed gifts in the church for the purpose of bringing the saints to spiritual maturity. The apostles have been given the ability to establish and *govern* churches. Prophets have been given the ability to instruct and *guide* people into God's purpose. The evangelists have been given the ability to *gather* the souls for Christ. Pastors are the shepherd's that *guard* the sheep and teachers have been given the ability to *ground* believers in the Word of God. It is important to become a member of a church that recognizes all of these gifts. Collectively, these gifts can help us grow up in God.[2]

Another spiritual transition occurs when a Christian becomes grounded in the Word, and begins to walk by faith and not by sight. That individual makes a transition from being carnally minded to spiritually minded. The spiritual man is lead by the Spirit of God and not by flesh. This person is learning or has learned to follow the leading of the Holy Spirit. His mind is being transformed and he is growing with full confidence in the Word. Spiritual maturity is also developed as we persevere through fiery trials and tests of our faith. Perseverance works to make us mature and complete in Christ.

> Consider it pure joy, my brothers, whenever you face trials of many kinds, because you know that the testing of your faith develops perseverance. Perseverance must finish its work so that you may be mature and complete, not lacking anything. — James 1:2-4

As we become more spiritually minded, we must continue on the path to develop Christ-like attributes. We experience many bumps in the road during our journey. We contend on a daily basis with heart issues that hinder us. Since God looks at the heart and knows our intentions and motives, it is important to keep our hearts open before Him. God knows us better than we know ourselves, because He searches out the inner most part of our being.[3]

The Spirit searches our heart and can show us exactly what's within us. However, we must be willing to drop our guards and receive correction. It is easy to point the finger at the other person or say the problem is someone else. It is so easy to say, "but God, what about me?" In some cases the other person may be at fault, but we are still accountable for our attitudes and actions. There will always be times when we struggle with having the "right" attitude or the "right" response. The good news is that the Spirit of God is available to assist us in conquering all heart issues.

The heart is the center of our soul and the seat of our affections. The soul is comprised of our mind (our intellect), our will (our choice), and our emotions (our feelings). Some people are led by their intellect, by what they think is right or wrong. While others are led by their feelings, they may not feel like doing a particular thing. On top of dealing with our intellect and emotions, we have to wrestle with

our wants and desires to make our will subject to the will of God. The world tells us "follow your heart," but the Word tells us "follow after God and to be led by the Spirit." To be truly honest, our hearts can lead us in the wrong direction if we aren't completely submitted to God. This is not to say that God will never give us the desires of our heart. Many times God will place His desires for us within our hearts so that we

might be drawn in a particular direction. The key here is to trust that God knows what is best for us.

In the book of Proverbs, we are encouraged to make guarding our hearts a top priority. We can link guarding our heart back to our priestly duties as described earlier in "The Pattern of Worship" chapter. The priests were charged to guard the gates to the sanctuary. Since we are priests under Jesus Christ, we are responsible for guarding the gates to the sanctuary of our hearts. In the vision of Ezekiel, there were gates located on the north, south, east, and west of the temple. We can imagine the north gate as our eyes, the east and west gates as our ears, and the south gate as our tongue or lips. Our eyes and ears are the openings to our soul; therefore, we must be careful to shut off things that will contaminate us.

Every life experience makes an imprint within our hearts. We store a wealth of information and experiences, some of which can go very deep. Whatever we see or hear is recorded in our subconscious memory, all of which can directly affect our motives, attitudes, actions, and words.

We must also guard what comes out of the south gate. It is out of the abundance of the heart that the mouth speaks (Matt. 12:34). Remember the *Tongue* that protrudes into the Dead Sea and divides it? Our tongue can cause division and take us down hill quickly. If we want to control what comes out of our south gate, we must control what comes into the other gates.

Ezekiel 44:5,7 strongly warns us to mark well and set our hearts to see with our eyes, and hear with our ears all that He said concerning the ordinances of the house of the Lord, and mark well and set our hearts to know who are allowed to enter the temple, and who are excluded from the sanctuary. Next, we are reminded how we can pollute the sanctuary of our hearts. "You brought foreigners uncircumcised in heart and flesh into My sanctuary, desecrating [to pollute and profane] My temple while you offered Me food, fat and blood, [and through it all in addition to all your abominations] you broke My covenant." This confirms how important it is for us to guard our hearts. One of the most effective methods of guarding our heart is reading, praying, and meditating on the Word of God. We should always process everything through the Word, because it is a safety net of protection.

Whenever I respond emotionally to the issues of life, I run quickly to the Lord for help. My burdens are always lightened after spending time in the Word, in prayer, or in praise and worship. I retreat to God whenever I am feeling anxious, challenged, competitive, or spiritually weak. No matter what the emotion, it is detected, arrested, and corrected by the power of God. This doesn't always mean that my problem has gone away or that my circumstances have changed. It does mean that my spirit is no longer vexed, and I can rest.

Spiritual Traits of the Heart

A spiritually mature individual will have evidence of the fruit of the Spirit growing in his life. The fruit of the Holy Spirit is the inherent characteristics of Jesus Christ. There are nine fruit of the Spirit: *love, joy, peace, patience, kindness, goodness, faithfulness, gentleness, and self-control.* In order for our character to reflect a mirror image of Christ, we must acquire those same distinguishing qualities. God desires that we bear GOOD fruit so that others will know that we belong to Him.

As our relationship with Christ grows, desirable fruit will develop. Apart from the true Vine, our fruit may look fine to the natural eye, but it will be rotten within. We wouldn't want people to look at us and think, "That child is just spoiled rotten." Jesus is our source of life and apart from Him there is no good fruit. As we remain connected to the Vine, God will prune us so that we may continue in our spiritual growth. Our goal is to become a mirror reflection of Jesus.

> I am the true vine, and my Father is the gardener. He cuts off every branch in me that bears no fruit, while every branch that does bear fruit he prunes so that it will be even more fruitful. — John 15:1-2

In comparing Galatians 5:-22-23 with 1 Corinthians 13, we see God's nature. As we look closely at these scriptures, we see the fruit of the Spirit is "love." First Corinthians 13:1-14 points out the characteristics that exemplify love. We should always refer back to these scriptures to make certain that we are walking in love, because anything we do without love is in vain. God gave me a poem entitled "Follow After Love." First, read the scriptures, and then refer to the poem to see the direct correlation of agape love and the fruit of the Spirit.

Follow After Love

Oh Love, oh love, how I desire to become more like thee
You have so many qualities that you can teach me
I sit and watch, observing as I do,
seeing all those things that are becoming of you
Everything about you, reflects the character of Jesus Christ
Oh Love, show me how to be that nice.
I see your patience, suffering long you do, oh how I long to be like you

It's sometimes so hard to wait on the promises and desires to come to pass
And therefore I can't help but ask,
"When Lord when?"
Do you ever ask that question my friend?
You are so strong; I need your strength so,
It is your Love I want to know

Love, you are kind to those around you,
both your loved ones and associates too
and this is during the times you are going through
Oh, how I follow after you.
You do not boast or act selfishly, nor is pride present in thee.
You are not self seeking, fulfilling the desires of the flesh
nor are you envious
Under certain conditions it's hard to hold my peace,
and the pressure inside I just want to release
But, as I follow after you Love, I am reminded of your way
And I'm challenged to keep trying day by day.
When you rejoice it is for truth and truth alone
And again I say you rejoice for truth and not for wrong

I admire you my Love, for you bear all things, you believe all things
Hopes all things and endures all things.
Love, you never fail. Oh, how I long to do these things as well.

Help me to know you and birth in me your great fruit,
Oh sweet love, it is you I salute
Love, as I stretch forth to become like the greater things of this life,
Which is walking in the love of my Lord, Jesus Christ.
I stretch down deep to become rooted more in you,
so that I may bear much good fruit
I also stretch myself wide, so in God's love I will abide.

For to love is to live and to live is to love
This love comes from God above
Let us strive to bear the fruit of the Spirit,
for the fruit of the Spirit is Love
Follow after Love my beloved, follow after Love

Examine the Issues of the Heart

If we don't have an understanding of our heart issues, we will never be able to draw them out to properly deal with them.[5] Our heart issues can sometimes be obscure and hard to understand. Thank God that we are not left without hope. God will turn on the light of our understanding, as we allow the Lamp of God to search our hearts.[6] Darkness resides where there is a lack of understanding, but the Spirit of God can enlighten our understanding if we seek the Word for answers. Remember, God desires to unveil truth within the sanctuary of our hearts. He removes the veil and brings understanding.

Jeremiah 17:9 declares that above all things, the heart is deceitful (having a **tendency** to be **dishonest or misleading)**. As long as we live in the flesh, there is a tendency to allow the sinful nature of the flesh to get the best of us. If we follow the flesh, our emotions can sometimes cause us to be deceitful. We don't want our ways to remind God of satan, the arch deceiver, whose mission is to deceive all. Let's not linger here. There are ways to help us resist those tendencies. We are not to give place to satan by allowing our anger to cause us to sin. We are to obey the Word of God, remembering to put on the whole armor of God so that we may be able to stand against the devil. We are to be self-controlled and

A walk of integrity as a believer in Christ is important. Spiritual maturity becomes even more important when we live a life as a minister. Our lives become like an opened book once God begins to use us as ministers. A minister is one who serves others in some capacity, which means that people are always watching our every move. People will watch our walk. They will watch what we say and do. They will watch our lifestyle. They will watch our attitude and our response to others. This is all the more reason for us to live a life submitted to God. Our walk should demonstrate Christ-likeness as much as possible. We all have areas within our lives where we fall short, but the grace of God is here to help us. But, as we become aware of our faults and weaknesses, we must submit them to the Lord immediately. God brings change in our lives whenever our hearts are willing, submitting those areas of concern to Him.

alert, standing firm in our faith. Since the tendency to be deceitful is a present factor, we can always pray. We can pray in the Spirit. The Spirit intercedes for us, praying the perfect will of God. We are to submit our minds, will, and emotions to God and resist the devil so that he will flee from us. We oppose satan whenever we declare the Word over our lives, understand the Word, and obey the Word. Once we recognize that we have a heart issue, we are to submit the challenge that we are facing to God.

Understanding the Issues and Seeing the Flaws

As a seamstress, I can usually tell whether a garment is of good quality based on the fabric and construction. In some cases, I know based strictly upon the name sewn inside or outside of it. A poor quality garment will not hold up under wear and tear, while a quality garment will have durability and longevity.

Our lives have been sewn together with our experiences (failures, successes, disappointments, and victories). In some areas, we have grown and matured, while in other areas we have suffered delay and arrested development. Those areas that lack spiritual maturity are like character flaws. A flaw in the fabric of a garment affects the quality. A seamstress will rip out the flawed section and replace it with flawless material. If that flawed section is not removed, the garment cannot be sold at full price. Likewise, as we abide in the Vine, God will work on the flawed parts of our character. We must allow Him to help rid us of them.

At times, it may feel like we are coming apart. This may be the hand of God with His seam ripper working to remove those flaws. It doesn't feel good when God pinpoints specific character flaws, but the end results are well worth the unraveling. Like a quality garment, God wants us to endure when the going gets tough. He wants us to give in to His way, bend, and be flexible.

Our lives have been sewn together with our experiences (failures, successes, disappointments, and victories).

God is "constructing" us to be patient, disciplined, faithful, and kind, while walking in love, joy, and humility. God is redefining our person. Be encouraged. Over time, we (as well as others) will be able to see what the workmanship of the Lord has done in our lives. All things will work together for our good as we trust in Him and leave our lives in the Master's Hands.

God doesn't have just one seam ripper, He has many. They come in all shapes and sizes. God will use people as seam rippers to remove the seams, stitch by stitch, until we can no longer hold it together. We lose control and God takes control. He knows exactly what it will take to get us to the point of surrender. He will get us to the point of saying, 'I don't know how,' then He'll say, 'I'll show you how.'

"Let us examine our ways and test them, and let us return to the Lord" (Lam. 3:40). We will never really know what is in our hearts until we either act or speak it out. Prophet Isaiah had a vision of the Lord's glory. The Lord was sitting on His throne high and lifted up as His train filled the temple. During the vision, Isaiah examined his ways and realized that He was a man of unclean lips. Then one of the seraphim flew to Isaiah and touched his lips with a hot coal from the altar of God. The fire of God purged away the iniquity and sin from Isaiah. The purification process cannot begin until we examine our ways and turn to the Lord for help.

It is written that no man can tame his tongue. I believe that Isaiah was speaking in regards to his tongue. Our tongue can be a deadly weapon, which is why we should control it and be careful with our words. In James chapter three, we are given powerful illustrations of the ability of the tongue. Our tongue is small like the rudder of a ship, but it has the power to determine the course that we take. It has the ability to build up or tear down, to bless or curse, and to provoke a fire or soothe a fire. Our tongue can cause deep wounds in others whenever we speak harshly. We must be sensitive to this fact by guarding our tongue just as we guard our heart. The heart and tongue are uniquely intertwined.

Above all else, guard your heart, for it is the wellspring of life.

—

Proverbs 4:23

The tongue speaks what the heart feels and the heart receives whatever the tongue speaks. There will be times when the pressure is on and we speak what we feel, bringing those things within our hearts to the surface. During those times, we must submit it to God. We are to speak according to the Word and not according to our circumstances. The words that we speak are seed. If we plant good seed, then we will reap well.

You may ask, how will I know what issues I have? There are probably already symptoms that can clue you in to a particular unpleasant behavior. Once you recognize and acknowledge the behavior, it's time to begin seeking God for understanding. Ask God to show you the depths of your heart. People usually don't know why they behave a certain way or what triggered the behavior. During your prayer, ask God to help you find the root cause of the behavior. Then begin with a scripture search. Ask the Holy Spirit to lead you through the process. You may find that your issue is deep, but just keep going deeper with your research on the different terms that relate to your behavior. Through your persistent faith and by the grace of God you will be able to walk out the process. With this search you will need more than the Bible and a dictionary. You will need a concordance with the Hebrew and Greek references to help deepen your level of understanding.

The purposes of a man's heart are deep waters, but a man of understanding draws them out.

—

Proverbs 20:5

My Personal Seam Ripper Experience

It started when the Spirit of God began to show me that my lack of patience with my husband stemmed from pride. He showed me that symptoms of anger and harshness of words would surface from time to time. I prayed about my pride issue and all of its symptoms, but they continued to show up. I didn't understand, so my search began.

My impatience was the character flaw that God was pinpointing. God wanted to rip out impatience so that I might acquire His patience. I thought the meaning of patience was knowing how to wait on God. Wrong! Having patience is a lot more than waiting, or taking your time with others, or in doing things. To be patient means to bear pains or trials calmly without complaint. It is manifesting forbearance under strain. Patience is not hasty. It is steadfast despite opposition or difficulty. Well, I thought I had some of those qualities, but I certainly didn't have them all. God wanted to show me that I still had plenty of room for spiritual growth. The impatience within my heart was magnified when my husband's job situation changed. The weight of responsibility for supporting our household was placed on me. It didn't affect me as much during the initial turn of events, but over two and a half years, the stitches started to come apart. My emotional pain and physical strain increased. Then I became intolerant of some of my husband's ways. I was frustrated with myself because I didn't like the way I was treating him. Some days I would come home from work and over look things that were not to my expectation. On other days, as soon as I entered the house, I would just lose it and go through the house on a cleaning rampage. I didn't understand why I became so easily angered with him. So, how does all of this relate to pride?

Well, during the initial stage of my search, I began to study the traits of a prideful heart. I researched all the scriptures on the term *pride*. God showed me that the pride in my heart relating to my husband began with comparison. Whenever we disagreed on an issue, I would formulate my opinion, compare it to my husband's opinion, and cast judgment. *Judgment* is the process of forming an opinion or evaluation by discerning or comparing.[7] This mental action was damaging because it resulted in me feeling resentment towards my husband whenever he did or did not do something my way. Those opinions were like a yoke around my mind and my mental attitude changed towards my husband. Then this new mindset became a stronghold. Now I understand why the Bible tells us not to judge others. I also began to complain a lot.

Let's take a look at the other symptoms I was having. There was anger, resentful thoughts, and *haughty resentful words*. Whenever these symptoms were triggered, I began to develop a strong dislike for either my husband's action or non-action. I began to *despise* certain ways of my husband, which resulted in my heart hardening. That hardness caused me to treat my husband differently. My words became harsh instead of gentle. As I became aware of my issue, I began to pray, asking God to remove the callus from my heart. I asked Him to again soften my heart towards my husband. God would then do an immediate work and remove the hardness. It would last for a while and my words would become softer towards him, but something strange started happening. Those unpleasant emotional symptoms would eventually return. I continued to seek God for help. Obviously, I was missing something. I was following the instructions in God's Word, which told me to examine my ways. I became an investigator of my own thoughts and actions, searching for the details that would lead me to truth.

I received more insight when I began to study the symptoms. The haughty resentful words would come whenever I was angry and spoke my mind. *Haughty* means to be blatantly and disdainfully *proud*.[8] Disdain refers to having feelings of contempt, and showing a lack respect or reverence for something.[9] In my case it was showing a lack of respect for my husband. I learned that my hot-tempered emotions and judgmental attitudes were disrespectful. This was a rude awakening for me. Once I gained this new understanding, I felt so embarrassed. Philippians 2:3 tells us *"let nothing be done in strife or vainglory; but in lowliness of mind* (humility) *let each esteem others better than themselves."* This verse is the epitome of respect. Even though I felt I could justify the reasons behind my thoughts, feelings, and reactions, God viewed it as prideful thoughts. It is good for us to discuss our feelings, but we need balance in our thinking so that we avoid establishing an unhealthy mindset about another person.

The Spirit of God opened the eyes of my understanding even more through Proverbs 15:4, which states that "the tongue that brings healing is a tree of life, but a *deceitful* tongue crushes the spirit." The King James Version of the Bible has the word *"perverse"* in the place of deceitful. *Peevishness* was the one particular definition

I learned that I must first look within if I wanted to understand why things were happening in my life.

of *perverse* that fit my symptoms. To be *peevish* means to be *cranky*, *querulous* in temperament or mood, fretful; and to be perversely *obstinate*, and marked by ill temper.[10] I started laughing uncontrollably when I discovered that these terms described my symptoms so well. A new freedom came inside me. Knowing the truth will set you free! I realized that my peevish, cranky, and querulous attitude towards my husband was the total opposite of patience. All the events that occurred to trigger my symptoms were part of God's hand pinpointing my character flaws. He was working to rip those flaws right out of me. Ouch! Since my initial understanding about patience was not complete, I would easily wound my husband with my words. My tongue would crush his spirit and cause him to shutdown. The things that my heart desired would not occur because I had started a vicious hurtful cycle. I would be hurt, then he would be hurt, and nothing would get accomplished unless I did it myself, which ultimately caused me to feel more weight and more pain.

After gaining more understanding about the root causes for my symptoms, God began to give me even greater insight. *"The purposes of a man's heart are deep waters, but a man of understanding draws them out"* (Prov. 20:5). The word "purposes" within this verse can be described in two ways. First, God foreknew us prior to our conception and has a divine plan awaiting us, to be walked out, lived, and fulfilled. He has already placed His purpose(s) for our lives deep within our hearts. However, we must first have understanding before we can see how to draw them out. We will never be able to walk in the fullness of what we've been purposed to do until we seek the mind of God for wisdom. Secondly, the purposes or circumstances surrounding our lives occur because of those things that are hidden within our hearts.[11]

With that revelation, I learned that I must first look within if I wanted to understand why things were happening in my life. My initial search on the symptoms lead me from one detail to the next, which all helped me to understand the reasons or purposes behind my deep issues

We should now know that as we search out the wisdom of God, He will lead us on the right path to attain the ultimate goal of growing in Love.

or circumstances. With each new understanding I went through the process of acceptance, confession, and repentance. Every time more truth was revealed and my understanding increased, I experienced brokenness and more humility entered into my heart. I also discovered that the process I went through was counted as an act of worship from God's perspective. God was actually working to increase His Love inside of my Heart.

As I grow in the fruit of the Spirit, I increase in God's unconditional love. The scripture tells us that love comes from a pure heart, a good conscience, and a sincere faith.[12] As we draw near to the Lord, His Spirit will do the work of the priest in the sanctuary of our heart. James 4:8 says, *"purify your hearts, you double-minded."* We are to polish our thoughts with the Word that breaks wrong mindsets, so that we may have clear understanding. We are to examine our attitudes so that He can purge our hearts of things that are not like Him and make us clean. We are to *examine* by inspecting and carefully inquiring to test the conditions of our heart. This will then allow us to have a good *conscience*, knowing that our intentions are right.

We should now know that as we search out the wisdom of God, He will lead us on the right path to attain the ultimate goal of growing in Love. We are to apply our hearts to understand since it is understanding that will guard us during those difficult times. We must first begin sowing the seed of the fruit that we desire to harvest in our lives. Prayer, praise and worship, and studying God's Word will keep His River of life flowing to us and through us. We will then become like the trees planted by the river (Ezekiel 47:7-12).

Pause for Prayer: Cultivate Our Hearts

Create in me a pure heart, O God. May the words of my mouth and the meditation of my heart be pleasing in Your sight. Help me to examine my ways, motives, attitudes, and actions. Purify my heart by the enlightenment of Your Word. Give me understanding concerning the depths of my heart so that I can be changed into Your likeness. Help me to become a true worshiper that you seek after. Allow Your fire, oh God, to refine me and purge me of those things that are not like You so that I may become a peacemaker; being gentle, pure, full of mercy and good fruits. In Jesus Name, Amen.[13]

Natural Traits of the Heart

> "When you reject the Word and do not put it into your heart and mind, the old nature assumes control—and you shut down the power and activity of your new heart."

> —

> *Juanita Bynum*[14]

We will end this chapter by reviewing some of our natural tendencies. As long as we live in these earthen vessels, our flesh will be contrary to the Spirit. Galatians 5:17 states, *"For the sinful nature desires what is contrary to the Spirit, and the Spirit what is contrary to the sinful nature. They are in conflict with each other so that you do not do what you want."* If we are **not** lead by the Spirit of God, the works of the flesh will manifest. We can be encouraged that according to Galatians 5:24-25, those belonging to Christ Jesus have crucified the sinful nature with its passions and desires. As we pick up our cross daily, we can crucify our emotions by submitting them to the Word of God.

If we are not exemplifying the character of Christ within our lives, then who are we imitating? Let's look at Lucifer's beginning. So often we start out with the right motives and intentions, but as you will see with Lucifer, his heart changed. Ezekiel 28:5-19 states Lucifer was created beautifully by the Master's hand. He was full of wisdom and perfect in splendor. Lucifer was anointed as a guardian cherub on the holy mountain of God, charged to lead and bring forth worship before the throne. He dwelt in the holy presence of God.

Lucifer was blameless in his ways from the day he was created until wickedness was found in him. His heart became proud on account of his beauty, and he corrupted his wisdom because of his splendor (Ezek 28:5-19). Therefore, God had him thrown out of heaven. From that point on Lucifer became satan, also known as the devil. The devil is still angry today because he lost his position in heaven. The believer must war constantly against satan and his ploys as he seeks to corrupt our minds with unkind, unworthy, and haughty thoughts, hoping that our hearts will become wicked like his. Every time the believer worships God, satan cringes because he knows praise and worship usher in God's presence where we receive peace, joy, and hope. We have taken his position in worship and he is jealous of every believer.

Now, what about praise? We have touched on the subject, but what does the Word of God say about praise? We are ready to progress to learning different ways to expressing praise and worship unto God. Let's clothe ourselves with spiritual garments of praise.

Some Emotions Experienced by the Heart

Nearly all scripture references on the heart refer to some aspect of our personality, character, and emotions.

ENVY
*A **heart** at peace gives life to the body, but **envy** rots the bones.* — Pro. 14:30

FEAR
*Say to those with **fearful hearts**, "Be strong, do not fear; your God will come, he will come with vengeance; with divine retribution he will come to save you.* — Isa. 35:4

JOY
*You have **filled my heart with greater joy** than when their grain and new wine abound.* — Ps. 4:7

LOVE
*Now that you have purified yourselves by obeying the truth so that you have **sincere love** for your brothers, love one another deeply, **from the heart**.* — 1 Pet. 1:22

PEACE
*A **heart at peace** gives life to the body, but envy rots the bones.* — Pro. 14:30

PRIDE
*Whoever slanders his neighbor in secret, him will I put to silence; whoever has haughty eyes and **a proud heart**, him will I not endure.* — Ps. 101:5

SINCERITY
*Surely God is good to Israel, to those who are **pure in heart**.* — Ps. 73:1

SORROW
*So the king asked me, "Why does your face look so sad when you are not ill? This can be nothing but **sadness of heart**." I was very much afraid.* — Neh 2:2

REBELLION
*But these people have stubborn and **rebellious hearts**; they have turned aside* — Jer. 5:23

Submitting Our Will to God's Way

What are we to do about our will? Instead of taking control, we are to lose control. We are to submit our will to God. We are to submit our will to those whom God has placed over us in positions of leadership. Learning to submit to leadership is all a part of growing in our spiritual maturity. To submit means to yield to the authority of another; to be subject to another. Submission is being submissive, humble, or compliant. There are great rewards in learning submission. According to Hebrews 12:9-11, righteousness, peace, and discipline are the rewards of a submitted life. In order to become a mature minister or leader, we must learn to submit to leadership.

There will be times over the course of our lives when leadership makes a decision that directly affects us. We must be careful not to react too quickly in those circumstances. Since God places leaders over us, we must trust Him with their decisions. If we oppose leadership, we may very well be opposing God. Our Father knows what is best for us. He cares for us and He will work things out for our good. If leadership has made a decision that is contrary to what God wants for us, God will intervene on our behalf. Submitting ourselves may cause us to have some mental or emotional pain, but as stated in 1 Peter 5:5-11, God Himself will restore us, and make us strong, firm, and steadfast. God will give us the strength to continue the course if we humble ourselves, submit, and trust Him. I do want to add a little balance here in saying that it is okay to share your heart when the door of opportunity opens, but we should always pray for guidance.

7: Praise Unlimited
Clothed with Spiritual Garments

During the crucifixion of Jesus, the soldiers removed the garments of Jesus from His body. The soldiers divided the outer garments among themselves. They then cast lots for the undergarment of Jesus because it had no seams, being woven from top to bottom. Jesus had both inner (undergarment) and outer garments covering Him. [1]

The church is now the spiritual Body of Jesus Christ. There are only a few mentions of spiritual garments in the Bible. They are *the robe of righteousness, the garments of salvation,* and *the garment of praise.* We, the Body of Christ, have been given inner and outer garments like our High Priest. The inner garment that could not be torn is our garment of salvation. The devil cannot tear salvation from us because Jesus made it available to us when He died on the cross. The inner garment of Jesus was not shared, but by an individual's faith, it is acquired. It is the garment of salvation. Salvation is a personal choice, and no one can accept Jesus as Savior for us. Jesus faced great humiliation when His undergarment was removed and His private parts were exposed. The blood of Jesus now covers those things that the enemy wishes to expose in our lives, and to counteract the condemnation that satan would bring, Jesus covered us in an outer garment, the robe of righteousness. Jesus allowed the enemy to take His robe so that we could wear it. We are now covered with Christ's "Robe of Righteousness." Salvation is like an undergarment, because it can't be seen with the physical eye. Righteousness is an outer garment that can be seen by others as we live according to God's standards. Jesus made all of these garments available to us. We are to put on all of these wonderful garments and wear them daily with confidence.

We have been given another outer garment called PRAISE. The outer garments of Jesus were torn and shared among the soldiers. Both righteousness and praise are outer garments that can be observed by others. St. Matthew 7:20 tells us that people will know us by our fruit. Righteousness and praise in our lives can yield good fruit that would be evident to others. Righteousness yields the fruit of the spirit. Praise is the fruit of our lips that can yield victory in every situation because praise touches the heart of God to move on our behalf.

The robes of the priest of old were designed with pomegranates of blue, purple, and scarlet along with pure gold bells sewn to the hems of their robes. This adornment was for two specific reasons; first to minister unto the Lord and lastly to be a sign to others. The bells were a sign of life. The people outside of the tabernacle knew that the priest was still alive as long as the sounds of the bells could be heard.[2]

I would like to add my own personal twist to the symbolism on the robes of the pomegranates, or passion fruit. We are now priest of the most-high God with the royal robes. The pomegranates symbolize praise. Praise is a word filled with action and expression. Our praise to God should be full of passion. Our praise should have a distinct smell to the nostrils of God. Our praise should be juicy and full of flavor. We want God to just "eat up our praise." We want Him to be pleased with our praise. Let's produce the passion fruit of praise with our lips, speaking words of love, adoration, and appreciation toward our Lord. We want others to know that we belong to God because we are always giving Him praise.

Praise is both a gift and a sacrifice that we offer to the Lord. When we offer up the sacrifice of praise, our flesh dies, and our minds are then elevated to a higher place so that we can focus and concentrate on God and all that He is to us.

We can think well of God, but true praise comes from our mouth. Regardless of how many wonderful thoughts

I delight greatly in the LORD; my soul rejoices in my God. For he has clothed me with garments of salvation and arrayed me in a robe of righteousness

—

Isaiah 61:10

we have towards God, if we don't ever open our mouth to express those thoughts, we are withholding praise from the one whom we adore. God truly does know our thoughts, but the words only count when we voice them. Look at it this way, whenever a bad thought comes into our mind we wouldn't want God to count that thought as sin against us would we? Our thoughts can move us in a negative direction or in the right direction. If we think too much on the wrong things, eventually we will carry them out. Likewise, if we meditate on the goodness of God, eventually our lips will begin to speak of His goodness, giving praise to His holy name. Hebrews 13: 15 states, by the fruit of our lips we are to praise God. The words that we speak are seed. Every time we give thanks with our mouth, we are watering those seeds, which will yield beautiful fruit of praise in our lives. Our environment will be transformed into praise. Many blessings will come our way. The manifestation of our victories will be the result of our praise and obedience to God.

> **Attitude Determines Altitude**
> The attitude of the leader sets the stage for those who are being led. The attitude of the leader can motivate, devastate, or disengage the student. When leaders are excited about what they do within the ministry and are excited about why they do what they do, then others will become motivated and become excited. Our attitude will determine our altitude!

Expressions of Praise

Praise is not limited to the words that we speak. We can express our worship in reverential movements as praise unto God. Let's take a trip into the Praise Unlimited Mall to learn more about the different types of praise. This mall will have an Israeli flare through the use of Hebrew terminology. I want you to use your imagination as we do a little "window shopping." Did you know that praise comes in all shapes and sizes? What fits me may not fit you, because we are unique individuals. We will be shopping for garments of praise. Let's see what looks good on us and fits us best. Who knows, as we go through you may try on something that you didn't think would fit you but it actually looks great on you. Now as we try on these garments, accept them and take them home. Then we can wear them whenever we want. Whenever we wear these garments to glorify the Father, He comes into our presence to admire the beauty of our praises to Him. Practically anything can happen when praises go forth.

TEHILLAH

Our first stop will be in the *tehillah* shop since it is the most familiar to everyone. *Tehillah* is the Hebrew word for singing songs of praise.[3] Everyone loves to shop at *tehillah* because most of us enjoy singing, even if we cannot carry a tune. We love to sing the melodies from our heart. We all have a unique voice, therefore everyone's *tehilla* will be a little different. In Acts 16, while Paul and Silas were in prison they prayed and sang praises to God. They put on the *tehillah* garment. Their praises were so wonderful to God that He began to perform wonders. The Almighty God began to flex His muscles and caused a powerful earthquake to occur, which shook the foundation of the prison and caused the prison doors to open. God didn't stop there. He caused everyone's bands to be loosed. Everyone in the prison was set free from bondage! Many of us are in spiritual prisons because of our past, our mind-sets, or present situations that bind us, but God can and will set us free as we learn to praise Him. The more we put on the garments of praise, the more opportunities will present themselves for God's anointing to come in and break those heavy bands that are holding us from moving forward in Him. God can loose us from any stronghold. He will deliver us from anything that tries to keep us bound and in bondage. The enemy wants to hold us down, but through praise, God sets us free. Know the truth and the truth will set you free; this truth will free you!

Wearing the *tehillah* garment won't only set us free, but God will also fight our battles. In 2 Chronicles 20:22-24, God sent out ambushes against the enemies of Judah in the battle of Jehosaphat. Jehosaphat was instructed to appoint the praisers to go before the army, and to sing and praise God while He fought the battle for them. The hand of God smote the enemy. Just imagine God's mighty hand moving swiftly with vengeance. The tribe of Judah experienced victory because God moved suddenly against their enemy. All they had to do was sing praises to God and the battle was won. We can experience similar victories as we obey God and as we praise Him.

TOWDAH

Now, let's stop in the *towdah* shop. *Towdah* is another garment of praise that we can put on with our lips or mouth, to give thanks to God. Thanksgiving comes from a heart filled with gratitude. *Towdah* should be a garment that is worn on a daily basis. Daily we can thank God for those things that are easily taken for granted such as another day of life, our salvation, His love, grace, mercy, and the list goes on. We must always remember to offer up *towdah* praise in conjunction with our prayers. The book of Psalms is filled with scriptures that exhort us to give thanks to God for His goodness and unfailing love towards us. Psalm 100:4 says it so well, *"Enter into his gates with thanksgiving, and into his courts with praise: be thankful unto him, and bless his name."* Anytime we go before God it should be done with a thanksgiving and praise.[4]

YAHDAH

Next door to *towdah* is the *yadah* praise shop. Both *towdah* and *yadah* come from the same principle root word, which means extended hands.[5] It is really beautiful when everyone in a congregation is wearing the *yadah* garment of praise, having lifted hands and yielded hearts to God. We transition our praise from the movement of our lips to the movement of our bodies. Whenever we lift up our arms and extend our hands towards the heavens we are opening ourselves up to receive from God. We open ourselves to be delivered from things that may be holding us bound. We open ourselves for healing to take place. We have all heard the saying, "action speaks louder than words." With *yadah* praise, we are speaking to God through our actions, through our movements. Our mouth may say, Lord I surrender all, but what is our body language saying? Extended hands say, Lord, I surrender. If you look at the example given earlier in the battle of Jehosaphat, can you imagine the praisers walking and singing holding their hands down by their side during the entire battle? Don't be too shy to wear the *yadah praise*. Just remember that God loves a yielded vessel and that you are opening yourself up for a blessing.

BARAK

Barak is another type of movement that positions us to receive from God. Through this form of praise, we bow our hearts to the Lord.[6] We bow down and lower our will and our pride. In Psalm 95, the psalmist exhorts us to worship and bow down before the Lord. In the same chapter we are asked to harden not our hearts so that we can hear God. As we bow down, our hearts are humbled so that we can hear from our maker. This is why traditionally whenever a person prays they will kneel before God. They position themselves to hear from Him. We might as well accept the *barak* garment of praise now and begin wearing it by choice, because as stated in Romans 14:11 and Philippians 2:10, every knee will bow before Jesus Christ and confess that He is Lord.

ZAMAR

Another familiar garment of praise is *zamar*, the stringed instruments.[7] *Zamar* praise produces the sound of music through the instruments. *Nelson's Illustrated Bible*

Dictionary gives a thorough definition of the instruments used by the Israeli people: "(1) stringed instruments, which used vibrating strings to make sounds; (2) percussion instruments, which were struck to produce musical sounds; and (3) wind instruments, which made sounds either by passing air over a vibrating reed or by forcing air through the instrument."[8] The harp or lyre is mentioned most in the Bible and next in line is the trumpet. Throughout the Old and New Testament we find words like, "sound of the trumpet, sound of cymbals, sound of the cornet, and sound of the organ."

Now *zamar* is most definitely a specialty shop. *Zamar* fits those best that are gifted, skilled, or trained to play the instruments. However, we don't have to feel left out, if we really want to wear this garment, we can pick an instrument and begin the training process. While waiting on a choice of instrument, we can always use the instruments that we were created with. We can use our mouthpiece to sing. We can use our hands to produce a percussive sound of praise by clapping. We can use our feet to jump, stump, run, and leap, all to give God praise.

The singers and the musicians were praising and thanking the Lord together, all on one accord. 2 Chronicles 5:13 says they made "one sound." Every singer and every instrument were in such harmony declaring the Lord's goodness. Something miraculous took place at the very moment they became one sound. The glory of God filled the house. Music is powerful, singing is powerful, and movement is powerful. As we learn to unify our gifts in worshipping God, the more we will experience the presence of God.

HALAL SHABACH

Praise Unlimited is filled with so much variety, but the mall might be closing soon so we must hurry to make it to all of the stores. The last two shops we will visit today are *halal* and *shabach*. *Halal* is a Hebrew word which means to celebrate or to be clamorous.[9] This type of praise is the total opposite of being quiet. It means to be loud and expressive which is very similar to *shabach* praise.[10] King David wore these garments well when he blessed God with a dance of celebration after the Ark was returned to its proper place. He declared in a loud tone the mighty acts of God. King David was so excited that he danced right out of his clothes. To the natural eyes he was almost naked, but to the eyes of God David was certainly covered by the garments of praise. I can almost picture King David jumping up and down, screaming, and shouting at the top of his lungs. He didn't care how he looked, nor did he care how he sounded. As king he wasn't even concerned about how undignified he appeared to the spectators. Have you ever wanted something to happen so much that when it finally did take place you just lost it? Well, that is exactly what happened with David. He just lost it and he could not hold his peace nor could he hold back his praise to God.

There are many other expressions of praise referenced in the Bible. You could do a word study by using *Strong's Exhaustive Concordance of the Bible*. Many of the Hebrew words related to physical movement are translated into English as "rejoice." Following is a table of terms to assist you in your "praise" word study.

Boast	Delight	Leap	Psalm
Bow (down)	Exalt	Lift (voice)	Rejoice
Celebrate	Glorify	Music	Shout
Clap	Honor	Play	Sing
Dance	Magnify	Proclaim	Testify

These terms can be incorporated in our praise through movement in the ministry of dance. Now, let's explore the "Word on Dance" and learn about the ministry of dance.

Helpful Hint

As we learn to unify our gifts in worshipping God,

the more we will experience the presence of God.

APPLICATION ELEMENTS

1: The Word On Dance
The Ministry of Dance

I t's time to rejoice and dance for the Lord is good and His mercy endures forever! God is faithful to complete the good work that He has already begun in us. We have covered the spiritual elements that are foundational to a lifestyle of worship. Now we will review the Biblical history of dance.

The components of praise and worship in movement are evident throughout the Bible. As stated in the preface, in the joy of the Lord we see the rivers clapping their hands moving in a circular formation while being dispersed from Eden, a place of pleasure and delight. As members of the Family of God, we find delight and great pleasure in the Lord. Our soul gives expressions in thought and feelings, while our body responds through words of praise and adoration, all of which can become visual through dance movements. With a pure heart, let us together release rivers of praise unto the King of Glory.

The "Word" on Dance

A dance of praise or worship is the physical or outward expression of the inward relationship or experience with the Lord. In her book, *Rejoice, A Biblical Study of the Dance*, Debbie Roberts states that dance is "the exact expression of the person doing the movement. Dance combines thoughts of the heart and motor combination to bring forth a structure of movement. As this structure takes form, it is called patterned movement or dance."[2] Patterned movement is the vehicle in which the inner experience can become an outward expression. Dance is a series of rhythmic and patterned bodily movements. To dance is to use technique, form, and expression to communicate to others our experience with the Lord. The Bible says that we are to show forth praises unto God. Dance is an avenue for us to show forth praises unto our worthy and Holy God.

Dance is an art form that has become more readily embraced by the Church. The enemy had stripped the Body of Christ of this form of expression; however, for more than twenty years the Church has been taking it back by force. From the beginning of time we were purposed to worship, and dance is one of the forms that we've chosen to accomplish the purpose. Through our experiences and personal relationship with Christ, we dance and we communicate through technique and movement. Movement will always enhance, enlarge, or add impact to what is being sung or played. Whenever we include enhancers in the dance piece such as flags, banners, streamers, praise hoops, etc., we add even more to the praise. More details on enhancers will be discussed later in the praise and props section.

> *"Dance is the visual and expressive part of worship."*
> — David Swan

Let them praise his name with dancing and make music to him with tambourine and harp.
— Psalm 149:3

An amazing thing happens when the people of God begin to praise Him. God is moved to come reside with us. Whenever God's divine presence is in our midst, anything can happen, from conviction to salvation, from healing to deliverance, from sorrow to joy, for God inhabits the praises of Israel. "Dancing unto the Lord brings you spiritual, emotional, and physical benefits. Physical movements help to release the emotions and with the release of emotions, the spirit is released. Anointed dancers thus have the power to liberate the atmosphere through dance. They can release the spirit of liberty and joy."[3]

Our vocabulary is so limited when it comes to describing such an awesome and almighty God. So often, we struggle to find the right words to describe or express our hearts to God. We may want to tell Him how wonderful or great He is and how much He means to us, but we become at a loss for words. Through movement we are able to demonstrate those expressions. As the adage states, action speaks louder than words. Dance frees our minds from the task of wondering what to say, we just allow our members to move. We bow, we bend, we leap, or we raise our hands. Our creator is more than worthy to be praised. His love and faithfulness towards us is so great. Psalm 150 exhorts us to praise the Lord for His acts of power and for His greatness that transcends all others. Everything that has life and breathes is to praise the Lord!

The Old Testament shows us that dance was an intricate part of the children of Israel's Hebrew tradition and culture. They used dance in worship, in ordinary life, in festive occasions, and during times of triumph and war. Many of their celebrations and festive occasions included circular ring dances or processionals. As seen in Psalm 42:4, they were led in a procession to the House of God with the voice of triumph and praise.

During times of exuberant joy, dance movements celebrated the occasion. After crossing the Red Sea, the children of Israel danced and rejoiced because Pharaoh's army drowned in the Red Sea. Miriam, the sister of Aaron, along with other women danced with timbrels in their hands. They praised their God for delivering them from Egypt. The scripture also states that the women sang as they danced declaring David's defeat of Goliath.

In his book, *Dancing for Joy, a Biblical Approach to Praise and Worship*, Rabbi Murray Silberling states, "Messianic dance is a part of the Jewish spiritual heritage. We express through dance the biblical roots of our faith in Messiah. Romans 11 says that the faith of our fathers, and the covenant He made with them, is the root by which the wild olive branches have become attached to something that is ancient and biblical. The Messiah, Yeshua, was born, ministered and gave His life for us in

"To Dance is to use technique, form, and expression to communicate to others our experiences with the Lord."
— *Debbie Roberts*

this context. It is important that Jewish and Israeli cultural expressions be a continual part of our praise and worship. Messianic dance is not just a Jewish phenomenon. It is a picture of the resurrection life of Yeshua expressed today in its biblical and historic context."[4]

Many passages referenced in the Old and New Testaments alluding to joy, rejoicing, or praise also implied dance. There are over 290 accounts of the term "rejoice" in the Bible. Rejoice is an action word meaning to give joy to or to feel joy with great delight. In our rejoicing, we react and respond to God with intense emotions and movement. In the parable of the prodigal son, there was dancing and rejoicing when the lost son returned home. Leaping for joy and rejoicing is shown in Luke 6:23. Jesus even commented about dance in Matthew 11:17, saying, *"We played the flute for you, and you did not dance."* God doesn't rule dance out of the church. It is supported by His written Word. Dance is like spiritual applause unto the Lord. Through dance, we take action, responding to God in movement with our entire body; in Him we live and move and have our being.

> **"During the 1906 Pentecostal** revival, the church world was shaken by what she saw; people dancing and rejoicing at the power and outpouring of the Holy Spirit. This is where we get our term "dancing in the Spirit." To the fundamental church this was offensive and certainly not of God. Other revivals had been stirring but this one so exploded it spread across America. True joy born by experiences of God came forth. This was a very emotional revival and the fundamental church rejected it as a manifestation of the flesh.
>
> Today dance is more readily being accepted in many churches. Denominational churches call it choir movement or drama. More liberal churches call it choreography and pageantry. Restoration churches call it Dance and recognize it as a ministry unto the Lord. Many churches have companies of dancers who minister in these areas. God intended his people to worship and praise Him. The Dance will grow in purpose and function as traditional bondages are broken."[1]
>
> — Debbie Roberts, Pioneer

Rejoice in that day and leap for joy, because great is your

reward in heaven. For that is how their fathers treated the prophets. — Luke 6:23

The supreme God Himself expresses His love and emotion towards us. He takes great delight in us and He rejoices over us with singing. It is so exciting to know that while the almighty God rejoices over us, He is giving His joy to us! No wonder we can say that the joy of the Lord is our strength, because it is truly divine joy activated within us that keeps us going.[5] During our times of sadness God will cheer us up and cause us to rejoice, birthing forth supernatural joy.

The LORD your God is with you, he is mighty to save. He will take great delight in you, he will quiet you with his love, He will rejoice over you with singing. — Zephaniah 3:17

Following is a word study on the term *dance* and *worship*. The word study includes both Hebrew and Greek terminology with scripture references for each definition.[6, 7, 8]

Hebrew Words	
Chwl or Chiyl	To twist or whirl in a circular or spiral manner, that is to dance, to writhe in pain or fear. Figuratively it means to wait, to pervert, to bear, bring forth and to make to dance, Judg. 21:21,23
Karar	To dance and to whirl, 2 Sam. 6:16
Machowl	A round dance, circle dancing, Ps. 149:3
Raqad	To stamp, that is to spring about wildly for joy, to dance, jump, leap or skip, Isa.13:21
Shachah	To worship by prostrating, bowing (self) down, falling down (flat), Deut. 26:10

Greek Words	
Agalliao	To jump for joy or rejoice greatly, Rev. 19:7
Choros	A round or ring dance, Luke 15:25
Latreuo	To minister to God, that is to render religious homage; to serve, to do service, to worship, Phil. 3:3
Orcheomai	To dance, Matt. 11:17
Proskuneo	To worship, to kiss (like a dog licking its master's hand), to prostrate oneself in homage, John 4:23
Skirtao	To skip, to jump for joy or to leap for joy, Luke 1:41

Other References for Dance in the Bible	
Dance of Dedication	Neh. 12:27; Jer. 31:4; Ps. 30:11
Dance of Deliverance	1 Chron. 15:16; 2 Chron. 20:15-25;Ps. 114:6
Dance of Praise and Worship	Pss. 30:11; 96:9; 149:2-3; 150:4
Dance of Restoration	Ps. 30:11; Jer. 31:4;Lam. 5:15
Dance of Reunion	Luke 15:11-31 (the prodigal son)
Dance of the Prophetic	1 Samuel 10:5-10
Dance of Victory	Exod. 15:20; 1 Sam. 29:5; 2 Sam. 6:5
Mourning Procession	Jer. 9:20; Luke 7:32
Processionals	Ps. 100:2-4; Judg. 11:34; 1Sam. 18:6;
The Dance of King David	2 Sam. 6:14-15; 1 Chron. 15:29
Wedding, Marriage, Courtship Dance	Song of Sol. 3:11;Isa. 61:10; Rev. 19:7

There is an enormous range of expressions in movement and dance forms, all of which can be offered in worship, from the carefully choreographed presentations to spontaneous praise. As individuals and as a congregation, let's present our praise as a celebration, rejoicing unto the King of kings and Lord of lords.

Understanding the Ministry of Dance

If there is a desire to dance for the Lord, God can take that desire and turn it into something beautiful. It is not necessary to be a trained dancer in order to worship and minister in Christian dance. While attending college, I was exposed to the dance ministry, and in 1989 I participated in my first dance with some college friends. It brought tears to my eyes when we ministered the dance for the first time during the church service. I could hardly believe that God gave back to me something that I had given up for Him when I became a Christian. Before accepting Christ as my personal savior, I enjoyed dancing. During my high school years, my friends and I would go to the teenage nightclub on Saturday nights, and I would dance all night. After my conversion, dance was the thing that I laid on the altar and gave up for Christ. I had no idea that I could dance for Him! I learned that my body was created for worship. I know it was God who planted the desire to dance within me.

In 1991, I was asked to lead a dance team in a church, and this was all without professional training. By faith I accepted. I just wanted to praise my Lord, and to express my love and gratitude to Him. God began to give me movements to express what my spirit man was feeling. As I listened to music in my home, I would see movements in my mind to express the words being sung. Sequence of movements began to form whenever I danced unto the Lord at home. Even during the church services, God would give me movements to express worship unto Him. These expressive movements can be called expressive worship dance or interpretive dance. Through this form of dance we express words in movement. Those watching can almost interpret the message being conveyed. God has used me in the dance ministry of interpretive dance for over 13 years. Intermittently over those years, I have been trained in ballet and other forms of dance. I wanted to learn more dance techniques to increase my skills.

In the scriptures, those who were called to help build the Tabernacle of Moses, the Tabernacle of David, and the Temple of Solomon were skilled in their trade. Studying our subject, getting the necessary training, and growing in skill is essential in becoming effective ministers in the areas to which we are called.

As ministers in dance, we must be sure that our motive in dancing is to minister to God, and to minister a word from God instead of dancing to perform so that people can see us and say how good we are. It is good to desire affirmation in the dance, but we must be careful not to let that become the motive of our dancing. Our motives should be based on Biblical truths. We dance to worship and praise God, to effectively war against satan, to minister the spoken word in visual form, to minister healing to the sick, to proclaim freedom to the captives, to bring joy to a sorrowed heart, to bring hope to the hopeless, and to break the yokes of bondage. God will anoint our dance for those very purposes.

Stir-up the Gift

Don't allow the lack of experience in dance to stop you from becoming a worship dancer. You can start off in expressive worship or interpretive dance and go from there, trusting God to bring increase in that area of your life. As you step out in the dance to test the waters, you will begin to stir up a gift that you didn't know you had. As you stir up your gift, your appetite for dance will increase. The gift will no longer be dormant, but alive and vibrant inside of you. You will be surprised where God might take you in the dance ministry. God will use what you have as you press forth in faith, progressing in excellence, growing in grace, skill, and ability.

Wherefore I put thee in remembrance that thou stir up the gift of God, which is in thee by the putting on of my hands. For God hath not given us the spirit of fear; but of power, and of love, and of a sound mind.
— 2 Timothy 1:6-7

As worshipers, servants, and as vessels we must know who we are in God. We are all called to be worshipers of the Lord Jesus Christ. Jesus Christ is the Anointed One. We who have accepted Jesus as our Lord and Savior are also anointed because the Spirit of Jesus, the anointed, lives inside each of us. Since the anointing resides in us by the Spirit, we are anointed to do whatever God calls us to do. We have all been called to worship; therefore, we are anointed to worship. One will never know that the anointing is within him until it is activated. When the anointing flows, the laboring goes.

The priest of old was anointed with oil, and the vessels within the tabernacle were also anointed, this indicated that they were consecrated and set apart for service unto the Lord. God instructed Moses to make holy anointing oil. This oil was composed of ingredients that were of both bitter and sweet in nature. There is both a bitter and sweet side in having the active anointing of God operate in our lives. We become acquainted with the bitter side when we experience the crushing process that is mentioned in chapter one. We are vessels desiring to be "used" by God. His hand will draw out His anointing. His hand will draw out those hidden treasures that are within us. Are we willing to pay the price? Remember, the olive must be crushed before the oil flows out, and before it can be effectively used.

On the sweet side, when God does begin to draw out the anointing, that which could not be seen will become stirred until our cup runs over. The anointing will flow out to bless others. It is the anointing that breaks the yokes. As we dance under the power and anointing of God, the anointing will begin to break yokes off those who are bound. God gives us supernatural ability and might (*dunamis*) to accomplish that which He has called us to do. The anointing breaks the natural boundaries that are present, and things begin to flow. If we are called to dance, God can turn our dance into ministry. God can use our dance to serve as an example of how we are to praise and worship Him. We must yield ourselves as available vessels to God so that He can use us to serve as ministers in the body of Christ.

There is an increased measure of anointing that God gives to those whom He calls to minister. We will refer to this increase as the "ministering anointing." This increased measure causes an individual to operate beyond their

Dunamis is the divine ability to do mighty wonderful work.[9]

natural limitations. It is almost like a tangible anointing that you can feel operating inside of you. You will recognize that it is God operating through you to minister to the people. The best way to describe this increase is to compare the experience to shifting a car into overdrive or increasing the gears on a bicycle. The amount of effort that one must induce to move forward is decreased when the gears are shifted in the right direction. After ministering under this type of anointing, one may feel physically weak, because the anointing literally goes out to the people to break yokes, to deliver, and to heal. Jesus knew that He had been touched by someone because virtue left from his body.[10] Likewise, virtue will leave our physical bodies as we minister under the anointing of God.

One other thing that is rarely discussed in regards to the anointing is that people are drawn towards the anointing. When the anointing is evident in our life, we will find that people will become attracted to us. Some may not understand and mistake it for physical attraction. This can be very dangerous for the person with the active anointing operating in their lives. The enemy could use that attraction to lure one into temptation or even into sin. Sadly enough, many ministers have fallen into sexual sin because of this very reason. It is important that we as ministers recognize this fact so that we will be able to recognize the attraction and draw our boundaries before things go too far. Flattery feels good to the flesh. Whenever there is an absence of an emotional or physical need, we are more likely to welcome the special attention because it temporarily fulfills the need. We must immediately take it to the Lord in prayer. We must let our souls cry out for help in the time of trouble. We need to be honest with God and tell Him about our struggle. As we submit the situation to God, He will provide a way of escape.

To be frank, satan hates anointed vessels. He will try any and everything to destroy us and to cut off our ministry. The enemy does not want us to fulfill our purpose, so he puts distractions all along our path. Thank God for a way of escape through the Word, through prayer and fasting, and through praise!

Heavenly Father, Thank You for Your anointing that resides inside of me by Your Spirit. Help me to always be conscience of Your anointing operating in my life. Help me to recognize it when others become attracted to me for the wrong reasons. Then help me to draw the proper boundaries so that I fall not into sin. Please allow Your anointing to accomplish the purpose in which it was given. Whether it is to break yokes, to give direction, or to establish truth, Lord let Your will be done. Please help me to resist temptation and help me to run quickly to Your throne of grace for instructions and for protection. Lord, help me not to misuse or abuse the anointing by taking advantage of others. And, help me to always be as wise as a serpent and as harmless as a dove. Keep me in Your love. I pray this in the name of Jesus. Amen.

God is no respecter of person in who He chooses to anoint for His service, but it is linked with faith, obedience, and relationship. God blesses those who obey Him and awakens the anointing in those who willingly seek after Him to know Him.

Helpful Hint

Don't become discouraged about your skill level. Allow God to take what you have and use it for His glory. Build your skill whenever the opportunity arises. Look for a local dance school to attend dance classes. Keep your eyes and ears opened for surrounding Christian Dance Conferences. Dance conferences can introduce you to a variety of dance styles and technique.

2: Ministry Mission

Developing a lifestyle of worship is a safety net for anyone who ministers in dance. Through that lifestyle, we learn how to conduct ourselves as ministers. We are to learn to serve and minister in the same capacity as Christ. Jesus told the disciples that they would do greater works since He was going to be with the Father.

God wants to do great things in us. God seeks after those through whom He can minister. God will minister through us by His Holy Spirit. God can take any gift and make it a ministry. Here we will discuss how one becomes a minister in dance.

As a minister in dance, it is important not to confuse ministry with performance. We are not to substitute ministry with performance, or entertainment. This is especially true when we are asked to dance at a family or community event. They may think that we are the entertainment, but we will know within our hearts that God has opened the door of opportunity for Him to minister through us. As a warning, we should never substitute having a heart for God for a heart for the art. We need to have a love for God and for the art in order to become effective ministers in the dance.

By definition, the term "dance" is a form of the performing arts, which involves bodily movements and human interaction. We see the performing arts demonstrated in theatrical plays, mime, music, and song. As the scripture states, there is a time and season for everything. There is a time for performance and there is a time for ministry. Performance is a familiar term to the world. The world can only teach us to perform. The world has etched a model of performance within our minds that we tend to model even within our Christian church settings, but as ministers in dance, we must understand the difference between the two terms, ministry and performance.

To perform is to demonstrate skill or ability, whether it is on a stage or in an office. On our secular jobs we are driven to perform. We are challenged to do our best so that we may reap the highest reward. That's the business world, and that's okay, in its own place. Everywhere you look there is performance. We see the stars of Hollywood performing all the time as they present their best to the audience. Their primary goal is to impress their audience. Performance to an audience is meant for entertainment and there is nothing wrong with good clean fun or good entertainment. We all enjoy watching a good wholesome movie, listening to a comedian with clean jokes, or even attending a classical or Christian music concert. We pay our money and expect excellent performance.

Lord, I am a vessel at Your disposal, use me to get Your message through to the people.

We understand how to perform, but how does one become a minister? Whenever an individual recognizes and comes to understand that his gifts were given to him by God to use for His glory, to minister to Him, and to serve others, then his mission in doing what he does changes. His attitude and motive will change. A minister no longer represents himself, but he is also an agent for God. He has yielded himself as an instrument for God's use. It is no longer about the art or the gift. The gift and ability are now focused on ministry instead of entertainment.

A minister's heart says, "Lord, how can I use this gift to glorify You, and to serve You and Your people? Lord, I am a vessel at Your disposal, use me to get Your message through to the people." A minister's heart desire is to reach the audience, not to impress with his skill and ability, but as ministry unto the Lord and to others. We learn that He is the one to be worshipped and not ourselves. Whenever this paradigm shift occurs in our minds, we will no longer want to just perform, but minister. Instead of rehearsing and worrying about the result, we should rehearse and pray about the result. The enemy will not be victorious in bringing discouragement just because we missed a step or movement, and though the enemy will certainly come to fill our minds with discouraging thoughts, we must recognize that it is satan coming to steal our joy. God turns it all around for the good and accomplishes His mission.

Now that we know that our mission is to serve, let's explore other attributes of a minister's heart. Several years ago while attending a seminar, the speaker, Lynn Haden founder of Dancing for Him Ministries, shared several points between a minister and a performer. I have taken some of those points and expanded them.

A minister prays before going before the people and puts his confidence in God, while a performer will put his confidence in himself, being determined to put his best foot forward regardless of the cost. A minister will take pleasure in ministering, because he can "direct the limelight to the Savior; a performer will enjoy performing because it puts him in the limelight." It is important to remember that Jesus Christ is the star of the show, and as ministers, we are to seek after an increased anointing in our lives and not after the applause. A minister sees himself as the "instrument," while a performer sees himself as the "master." A performer has a heart for the performing art, while a minister has a heart for God and the art. The fine line between the two terms performer and minister is really magnified when there is dissension. A minister would rather sit down than compete, while a performer will compete to be the best and will not sit down. "A minister will make sacrifices to further the ministry," while "a performer will make sacrifices for the good of his career." "Our greatest reward comes from God," not from men. We seek the kingdom of God first, believing He will supply all our needs, rewards, and compensation. We must always remember that as we keep our focus on God, keep Him first, all other things such as financial prosperity will certainly come.

We who have the higher calling to serve and to minister should aspire to carry out that calling with

A minister's heart says, "Lord, how can I use this gift to glorify You, and to serve You and Your people?"

excellence. *As ministers we should perform with the intent to minister.* We are instruments in the Master's hand. In the end, He is the Master Performer and all Glory goes to Him. He alone can yield true results and bring forth increase. We must always aspire to minister with our whole heart unto the Lord, and He will minister back to us and to others.

Romans 12:1 tell us to present our bodies as a living sacrifice unto the Lord. The word "present" means to bring as a gift before the King. As we dance before the Lord and minister unto the Him, we are presenting ourselves as a gift. We are not performing for the Lord, but we are presenting ourselves to Him. Whenever we dance in a staged setting before an audience, we may refer to it as a *presentation* rather than a performance. However, the majority of people will refer to our dance as a performance. Whenever given the opportunity we can always explain the difference between performance and presentation.

Now we will review two examples in the Bible of a dancer's mission and motive. The first example reflects a performance with a negative mission and a negative outcome. Mark chapter six gives us an account of Herodias and her daughter. The daughter's mission was to perform a seductive dance before King Herod. She danced to please the flesh of man. The motive of her heart was clear and was probably exemplified through her suggestive movements. Certain movements can cause people's minds to go south, right down the gutter. The young woman's dance pleased Herod so much that he was ready to give her whatever she requested. In order to satisfy her mother's wishes, she asked for the head of John the Baptist. The king granted her request. What a fatal ending![1]

This is an extreme example, but is being shared to show that our dance movements can be taken the wrong way. We must always be selective in choosing dance movements in order to minister. We want the intent of our dance to be viewed as ministry.

Our second example shows that the intent of Miriam's dance was for good. It was to celebrate and to minister unto the King of kings. Miriam was a prophetess and she danced prophetically in a spontaneous fashion to demonstrate their deliverance from Egypt and crossing the Red Sea. All of the other women followed her in the dance movements. They all had a glorious time celebrating the Lord![2]

Misunderstandings in Dance Ministry

Challenges will always occur in ministry, but we are not always prepared when the intent of our dance is misunderstood. Usually misunderstanding occurs when there is a lack of knowledge in regards to the type of dance being presented, or misunderstanding will happen when there is a lack of understanding concerning the intent of our dance. If anyone ever discloses disapproval to us concerning a movement, style, or expression then we must take the matter to God immediately. Only God knows the intentions of our heart and He alone can clear up misunderstandings. Personally, I had to learn to distinguish between that which was acceptable to God during my private worship time and that which was acceptable to man in a public forum. The intent of our heart could be very sincere when we express ourselves freely before the Lord. On the other hand, our expressions could still be misunderstood and become offensive. This is not to say that we quench the Spirit and withhold our praise and expressions to the Lord, but it does say that we should pray for God's wisdom in everything.

Misunderstandings in the dance can also occur when there is a lack of familiarity with a certain form of dance. The best example that I can use to help explain this point is when I was first introduced to African dance in the church. Our dance team was preparing for a dance conference and I was asked to help teach the African dance movement class. Initially, because of my lack of understanding and lack of familiarity with that form of dance, I wanted to reject the task in my heart. My understanding in the broadness of expressions in dance was extremely limited at that time. I wanted to remain in my comfort zone and stick to the forms of dance with which I was familiar. Up to that point in my life the ministry of dance consisted of only ballet, interpretive dance, and expressive worship. I prayed about my assignment and then told God that I would do whatever the leader needed me to do to help make our dance conference successful. I am so glad that I trusted God and followed through with my assignment.

I was allowed to explore a whole new world in dance expression and movement. God gave me more tools with which to worship Him. Through that experience I learned that African dance was fun and had exhilarating movements all of which could be used to express joy, thanksgiving, and praise to our Lord. I studied the history of this form of dance and was able to celebrate the Lord in a new way.

Our church congregation reflects the nations within the Kingdom of God, thus as ministers in the dance our movements and expressions to the Lord can be more versatile to show forth the glory of His Kingdom. As we lift up the Lord in our dance movements, He will draw all men unto Himself.

Whenever God speaks through our dance to the hearts of the people, they are usually moved or strongly impacted by the anointing of God. If there is unfamiliarity concerning the anointing and how God can touch our heart, an individual may become drawn, or physically attracted to the minister of dance, when in actuality God is drawing that person to Himself. The scripture to remember here is John 12: 32 which says, *"If I be lifted up, I will draw all men unto Me."* When we lift up the name of Jesus in our dance, the anointing of the Lord draws the people to Himself. To help curb any misunderstandings it is extremely important to always pray before going before people to minister. We must remind ourselves that we are ambassadors for Jesus Christ and we are to direct people to Him, instructing them to the Word and to prayer.

Our Heart Matters to God

Our dance team was going through a major transition and all the dancers were being assigned new roles. When I was told my position, my heart dropped. It was not what I expected, but God spoke to my heart immediately, and told me to accept it. As I submitted to the decision of leadership, God reassured me that it was His hand using the hand of man to direct my path. During this time, God honed in on my attitude. I had to make a decision to worship the Lord with all my heart regardless of the outcome. I had humbled myself under God's hand and felt complete peace. I was filled with an even greater joy.

Very shortly after that experience, a major blessing came my way. My friend called me to say that Juanita Bynum's ministry was looking for dancers for their upcoming Weapon's of Power Conference. I immediately went to the Juanita Bynum website to get a contact phone number. I was able to speak with one of the coordinators for the conference. She asked me how I acquired the information about the auditions since they had taken place two weeks earlier. She then asked me if I had a video of me dancing. I told her I would have my husband videotape me dancing at home. The coordinator told me that the dance choreographer preferred to see the dancers audition at the same time and location. She would contact her to see if she would accept my dance video. To my surprise, the choreographer agreed to accept my video. While my husband videotaped me dancing, my hand hit a mirror standing on an easel in our living room. I did not stop. I continued to worship the Lord through the remainder of the song.

A few days after I mailed the videotape, the conference choreographer called. She told me that she was very blessed by my worship to the Lord. She also reminded me of my mistake on the video. She told me that it was a good mistake because I kept dancing. She was looking for worshipers who would continue to flow regardless of the distraction. I was accepted as one of the conference dancers. I could hardly believe my ears! Everything was happening so fast. I was on my way to participate in a huge conference. Besides this event not being in my plans, it wasn't even on my radar screen. I never saw it coming. This was definitely the hand of God moving in my favor.

I had to believe God for the provision to go on the ten-day trip to St. Louis. Frequent flier miles covered my airline ticket. While sharing my testimony with others, God laid it on the heart of some to give towards my trip. I was given enough to cover my food and a portion of my hotel fees.

My husband and three sons sent me off with kisses and hugs. Once I arrived in St. Louis, I was greeted by the other dancers. After seeing the large number of dancers, I began to think that every dancer that auditioned was probably accepted. About half way into the first week of my trip I found out differently. I was informed that many dancers had been turned down during the audition. Solemnly humbled by the awesomeness of God, I thanked Him once again for choosing me to participate in the event.

During our stay, we learned many dances and spent hours in rehearsals. Our rehearsal times were not just practice driven, but they were heart driven. God used each session to prepare our hearts for worship. Many of us desired key roles for each dance. God tested our hearts and our motives for being there. Were we there to worship Him or to make a name for ourselves? The Spirit of God moved during those sessions. Some were even filled with the Spirit for the first time with evidence of speaking in tongues. There wasn't a dull moment. I had the opportunity to bond with several dancers during my stay.

Excitement and anticipation filled the air throughout the conference. The response of the people to God was incredible. There was an overflow of the anointing into the streets and hotels. People worshipped God in the lobby areas. People were praying and prophesying as we walked the sidewalks back to our hotels. We were in awe as we saw and even had the opportunity to join in on a prayer that took place in the hotel lobby.

At the end of the conference during our check out process my roommates and I were pleasantly surprised to find our bill paid in full! I checked with the hotel attendant to see if they made a mistake and charged the room fees to my credit card. No mistake, an anonymous person had paid the bill for all of us. We began to shout, 'glory to God, thank You Jesus!' God had paid for my entire trip! He had the vision and He provided provision. He told me before leaving for my trip that He would bless me from here to there, and He did just that! If we humble ourselves, in due season, He will exalt us and use us for His glory.

3: Technical Methods
For The Ministry Of Dance

Within the last few chapters, we have grown in scriptural knowledge relating to dance. We now recognize the foundational elements that help to establish a ministry after God's own heart. We should now be able to answer the questions, "Why we do, and what we do through the ministry of dance?"

We should not stop there. We need to understand the different dance styles or methods that we can apply within our dances. Applying the scriptural knowledge of movements to ministry with methods and styles of dance helps to create a well-rounded dance ministry. This chapter will help us transition from ministry to methods. The chosen descriptions give a basic overview of most of the dances that are available to us in this 21st Century. We will later cover two of those methods or dance styles in more detail.

Maintaining or Becoming Skilled

Many times throughout the scriptures we observe God calling forth those who are skilled in their craft for the building of the tabernacle and temple. He filled their hearts with wisdom, and with a willing heart they came to dedicate their skills and service unto the Lord. God always equips those He calls to serve.[1]

So Bezalel, Oholiab and every skilled person to whom the LORD has given skill and ability to know how to carry out all the work of constructing the sanctuary are to do the work just as the LORD has commanded. — Exodus 36:1

If you have a desire within your heart to dance and minister unto the Lord, then that may be your sign that He is drawing you to that area. You may think to yourself that God has not given you the skill or ability to dance. The seed of faith, believing that you can do all things through Jesus Christ who strengthens you, and the work of consistent practice with determination can yield the fruit of being skilled. If you find you cannot sit or stay still during praise and worship because you enjoy expressing your worship unto God in movement, then look a little closer, because dance may be the area in which you should become more skilled.

I encourage each person to enroll in a dance class in a dance school to help build technique and skill. As you grow, it is important to continue down a path of discipline, consistency, and practice. Practice helps to build and maintain technique. You become dull when practice is neglected. The dance techniques are what define the dance movement of the hands, arms, legs, feet, head, and torso. We are to express and emphasize our movements. There must be distinction in the movements to help convey the message. We can relate this to the musician who plays an instrument without clear note distinction; the tune being played would not be clearly understood. As dancers, we need to punctuate when necessary and convey a clear message.

Even in the case of lifeless things that make sounds, such as the flute or harp, how will anyone know what tune is being played unless there is a distinction in the notes?
— 1 Corinthians 14:7

You may think that there is no hope if you are not naturally talented or gifted in dance. There is nothing wrong with being trained to dance. The professionals are trained all the time to become the best. As Christians, we want to aim for excellence in everything we do. We want to offer God our best, not a lame sacrifice. Even when God was looking for maidens to wail over the people, He called for the skilled.[2] Then He encouraged those who where skilled to teach and train the younger women. How much more do you think He would want us to build our skill in the area of dance to worship before Him, and before His people?

We serve the King of kings. Therefore, we want to serve with all our heart and do it with excellence. As we begin to focus more on building our skill and dance technique, it is important not to lose focus of the most important areas of our lives and ministry, which is keeping a pure heart and a love relationship with Jesus Christ. We must pray for God to help us maintain balance in our life, so that we don't go overboard building skill and forget about building character. It is not always the skill, but the anointing at the right moment that makes the greater difference. The anointing comes through spending time with God, and through the process of being pressed from time to time during our test, fiery trials, and spiritual storms. Building that relationship with Jesus Christ should always be our primary focus!

Let's review the different styles of dance that are available to us today. Todd Farley, master of mime, addresses dance within his book, *The Silent Prophet.* "There is no form of dance which is higher than another; Israeli folk dance is no better than ballet or jazz. Although some dance forms lend themselves easier to the expression of worship, all forms can be used."[3]

Do you see a man skilled in his work? He will serve before kings; he will not serve before obscure men.
— Proverbs 22:29

Forms of Dance in the 21ˢᵗ Century

African dance originates from Africa. The people of Africa incorporated dance in their ceremonial celebrations. Drawing from their experiences, they expressed their beliefs of faith through their dance. Their dance rituals were demonstrated during religious ceremonies such as weddings, burials, and other spiritual occasions. Many of their dances signified practical daily activities such as hunting and fishing. Movements such as the wind, the rain, and animals were also incorporated in their dance rituals signifying nature and the natural elements surrounding them. Various types of dances reflect the different African tribes. African dance culture and art migrated with the people. African dance has become a form of art in North America, and is taught as another learned dance technique. Any ethnic group or individual can now enjoy this form of dance. The bodily movements are extremely rhythmic, energetic, and agile. Many of the African dances include foot shuffling and stomping, rapid arm motion, jumps, bends, swaying of the hips, and flexible torso movements all demonstrating plantation life, survival, and nature. The flow of each movement is heavily dependant upon the music. The drum or other percussion instruments are generally the dominant sound heard in African music. The African dancer will generally wear dance attire that reflects the African culture.

Ballet originated in Europe. This form of dance requires discipline and well-defined body training. It is a conventional dance where poses and steps are combined. The movements are more rigid and precise, but fluid in nature. The legs and feet are usually in a turned-out position. Turns and leaps are incorporated to assist in the fluidity of the dance. The movement and positing of the arms, feet, and head are extremely significant in the effect of the dance. Ballet is a dance style that reflects elegance, grace, and sophistication. Classical Ballet has its own terminology for each dance position and movement. These terminologies have been adopted by other styles and forms of dance. Gail Grant defines ballet as "a theatrical work or entertainment in which a choreographer has expressed his idea in group and solo dancing to a musical accompaniment with appropriate costumes, scenery and lighting."[4] Ballet is viewed as a foundation to begin learning dance technique and balance. It is also the most celebrated style of dance in the religious community.

*D*avidic sometimes called Messianic dance, incorporates "many elements of traditional Hasidic dance, as well as Israeli and Yemenite folk dances."[5] These circle dances are religious and ceremonial in nature and have "become the foundation of Messianic circle dances."[6] Davidic dance is carried out during social settings such as weddings, family gatherings, and during religious synagogue activities. This style of dance requires more than one dancer at a time and is more fitting for group circle dances. Davidic dance does not require technical movement, but generally incorporates easy steps such as, skipping, running, jumping, and moving side to side. Murray Silberling, the "dancing Rabbi," said, "Even at the beginners level, you can learn enough of the basic dances to immediately participate fully in the praise and worship."[7]

Expressive Worship incorporates dance movements that communicate the words in a song, and different levels of feelings and emotions derived from the words and music in a song. Expressive worship is nonrestrictive in the sense that it encourages freestyle movements. All forms of dance can be utilized to convey the message. This it is not limited to a specific style of dance. Expressive worship is often passionate in nature and can be done individually or in group worship. The dance becomes a more personal style of expression reflecting the dancer's adoration and love towards God. Sign language can be incorporated to emphasize certain words. Praise enhancers can be used to assist in the delivery of the message. Likewise, the dance garments can vary in style and color to reflect the theme, mood, emotions, or message of the song.

Hip Hop began as a cultural movement among urban youth (primarily African American) in New York and has since spread around the world. It requires movements that are upbeat and high in energy. The dancer must have a good sense of timing and rhythm to progress in this form of movement. It is generally practiced by the young at heart. Mime style movements can be incorporated into hip hop, to give a dramatic appearance. This dance includes forms of expression such as break dancing, stepping, sliding, and popping and locking the limbs. The dress style for hip hop is usually casual clothing and tennis shoes, conveying a very cool and relaxed look.[8] Hip Hop is used in ministry to help evangelize youth.

Interpretive dance can be religious or secular, and unlike expressive worship that is limited to religious exercise and belief, interpretive dance can incorporate many other forms of dance movements that are useful in relaying a message. In ministry, the term expressive worship, praise dance, and interpretive dance all melt together. Technically, however, interpretive dance is a form of modern dance in which the dancer's movements tell a story, preaches, paints a picture, or literally (through sign language) speaks the words of the song being played. It is purposed to yield a clear message to those who are observing the expressions. Sign language can be incorporated to add emphasis, drama, and meaning. This style dance can be learned without a lot of dance skill. It does require, however, the ability to convey a word, picture, or message through movement. The dancer's attire often reflects the message being portrayed.

Jazz is often theatrical and dramatic in presentation where the hands and fingers are extended. Jazz has its roots in tap and ballet. The movements are smooth, and the footwork is fast but accurate. The flexibility of the torso plays a significant part in this form of dance. Big and exaggerated movements with the individual body parts, such as the head, shoulders, hands, and feet are used to emphasize mood, transition, or ending. Costuming may vary from fitting to loose style clothing with jazz styled shoes, and can be coordinated with props such as hats, gloves, mask, or whatever that is appropriate to complete the delivery.

Modern dance is not a specific style of dance nor uses a single technical method of movement. Modern dance uses natural movements that are distinct from both ballet and jazz. The feet are normally placed in parallel position and the body held in balance. The movements are flowing and filled with expressive gestures. The dancer's movements often tell a story, but may simply convey a feeling. Unlike interpretive and expressive dance, modern dance is often choreographed and performed within a group. The dancer's attire and use of props reflect the message being portrayed. [9]

Prophetic dance may be spontaneous or pre-planned (choreographed). [10] "This type of dance is Holy Spirit inspired." [11] The dancer flows with the moment while the body movements and expression prophesy a message or paint a picture. The gift of prophecy is being administered through movement in prophetic dance. A prophetic dancer will often see the movements and then dance them out. No specific dance skill or technique is required in  the prophetic, only the ability to convey a message with movement is necessary. This form of dance is strictly done by faith, and the dancer must first step out in faith in whatever small part he sees, feels, or hears and then trust God for the outcome. Many times props are used to underscore the message.

Warfare dance is intended to convey the strength and might of God standing in defense of the  believer while upholding victory on his behalf. This type of dance also displays courage, determination, faith, and trust in walking out the victory. Warfare dance "as well as the praise dance, is used to prepare the atmosphere for the preaching of the Word."[12] This form of dance is done by faith, believing God to defeat the enemy, believing God for breakthrough, and for the continued victory that has already been gained through the blood of Jesus Christ. The dancer incorporates forceful arm and feet movements such as stomping the feet, twirling the body, and stretching the arms upward and as if pulling down strongholds.

Although all of the defined dance styles can be incorporated in the ministry of dance, "caution must be exercised whenever the movements are administered. Certain movements would not be acceptable in ministry. For example, too much hip movement would be a distraction. All dance movements in ministry must be directed towards God."[13]

As stated in Hebrews 11:1, faith is the evidence of things hoped for and the substance of things not seen. It is our hope, as ministers in dance, that God will manifest His power and anointing to bring healing, deliverance, and encouragement to His people. As ministers to and for God, we want to see people saved and set free.

Helpful Hint

Use basic ballet steps as a foundation for worship dance. Incorporate sign language and praise enhancers whenever possible to help convey the message or to add emphasis.

4: Spiritual Warfare And Winning Battles

Spiritual growth and readiness for worship through movement have been emphasized up to this point. It's time now for us to recognize the vastness of the spiritual world and understand that spiritual warfare is real. We do not want to become causalities in a spiritual battle. So where do we go and to whom do we turn?

God holds the times and seasons for all things in His hand. There is a need for an increased awareness of the physical and spiritual worlds, so that more victories can be won. There is a constant battle in the spiritual realm. Evil lurks at a distance, but it has no victory over God's people as we walk in divine authority. He who is in us is greater than any enemy in this world. No weapon formed against us shall prosper. As darkness covers the earth, the intensity of the light of God will shine through us to penetrate the darkness.[1]

> For God, who said, "Let light shine out of darkness," made his light shine in our hearts to give us the light of the knowledge of the glory of God in the face of Christ.
> — 2 Corinthians 4:6

Spiritual Warfare

Who is our enemy? Why does this enemy fight us? How can we win the battle and have victory? The scriptures unfold to us strategies to defeat the enemy. As soldiers in God's army we must stand, take our place, and effectively use our spiritual weapons of warfare! We must remember the words of Jahaziel in 2 Chronicles 20:10, *"the battle is not ours, but God's,"* for our battle is not with flesh and blood.

Revelation 12 makes it clear to us that our enemy is not of the flesh. Our enemy is a spirit-being full of spiritual wickedness. This enemy is the ruler of the darkness that we all see happening in this world. The dragon is that old serpent called the devil or satan. The devil was cast down to the earth along with his angel friends that supported him. In his anger of losing the heavenly battle he still wars with God's seed today. The vicious plan of satan is to deceive the whole world. He is out to make war with anyone who keeps the commandments of God and who has the Testimony of Jesus Christ. A part of satan's defeat was declared in the book of Genesis when he was told that the seed of a woman would bruise his head. Jesus Christ is the champion that dealt satan a final blow to the head by committing Himself to the cross and dying to redeem all mankind. The enemy's goal now is to destroy the remnant seed. There are principalities and spiritual powers in the heavenly realm used to war against us, but we are not to fear because God is with us.[2]

Weapons of Warfare

Anytime there is war, there are also soldiers. We are soldiers in God's army and He has equipped us for battle. It is not by might, nor by power, but by My Spirit declares the Lord. The Spirit of God leads, guides, teaches, and helps us to win. The weapons we fight with are not weapons of the world; they are spiritual. We've been equipped with the proper armor and weapons so that we might overcome in the midst of a spiritual battle. Our spiritual weapons can demolish the strongholds of the enemy. Through them we can cast down every thought that is contrary to God's Word.[3]

We have been given the whole armor of God as a safety net, which is purposed to cover us from the top of our heads to the soles of our feet. There are seven pieces to this armor that we are to apply to our life daily to help us to stand strong against all strategies and attacks of satan.[4]

Pause for Prayer

Father, right now I put on the helmet of salvation to protect my mind, to guard my thoughts and to cover my ears so that I might accept only words and thoughts that are aligned with Your Word. I put on the breastplate of righteousness to guard my heart and emotions so that I might walk in your love and righteousness. I also gird up my loins with the belt of truth, trusting and believing in Your Word and promises as it protects me from having a wounded spirit. Next, I shod my feet with the preparation of the gospel of peace so that I might walk in Your Peace even during moments of uncertainty, and be led by Your Peace. I hold up the shield of faith to quench every lie and attack of the enemy. I grip the sword of the Spirit, Your divine Word and truth as I study and meditate, so that I can use it effectively against the enemy. Help me also to be watchful in prayer for others and myself. I am thankful for the Blood of Jesus that covers me. Thank You for Your added hedge of protection. I pray all of this in the Name of Jesus. Amen.

This is an excellent prayer to start your day. While praying this prayer, act it out as if you were actually putting on each piece of the armor. Place your hands over your head and ears as you pray about the helmet of salvation. Motion your hands as if you're buckling a belt around your waist when you pray about your loins being girded with truth. Continue in this manner until you have put on every piece of your armor. These movements can be added to your dance vocabulary.

God is calling all of His soldiers to pull out and use praise as a major weapon of warfare. Whenever it seems that one or more parts of the armor are not fitting right and you feel like you're being defeated, it's time for praise. Maybe you are struggling to walk in the peace of God, or you war in your mind with wrong thoughts. Then use your weapon of praise. Maybe you are feeling from the words of a friend that the enemy succeeded in getting one of those fiery darts through to wound your spirit, then it's time to use your weapon of praise. Maybe you're beginning to doubt God's promises, then it's time for praise. Begin to praise God, telling Him how wonderful He is, speaking of His strength, mighty works, faithfulness, loving kindness, grace, and mercy. Begin to sing to Him, clap you hands or leap before Him, bow, kneel or lay before Him. Activate your praise missile and launch it in the face of the enemy, and guess whose presence will enter to fight for you, the King of glory, the Lord mighty in battle.

> Who is this King of glory? The LORD strong and mighty, the LORD mighty in battle. Lift up your heads, O you gates; lift them up, you ancient doors, that the King of glory may come in. — Psalms 24:8-9

Now that we have our armor and weapons of warfare and understand its use, how are we certain that it really works? Well, it's always nice to have a living example to demonstrate for us. We will now examine five different battles to demonstrate application and prove the effectiveness of our spiritual armor and weapons.

Winning Battles

As you read each battle, look for the keys to victory.

Battle 1: Exodus 17:5-13

Joshua fights the Amalekites as commanded. Moses stood on the hillside watching the battle with a rod in his hands. As long as Moses held up his hands, the Israelites were winning, but whenever he lowered his hands, the Amalekites were winning. When the arms of Moses became heavy and tired, Aaron and Hur put a rock under Moses for him to sit on and then each held up one arm of Moses. The Amalekite army was defeated. **The arms of Moses were extended upward as in Yadah praise.**

Even though I walk through the valley of the shadow of

death, I will fear no evil, for you are with me; your rod and your staff, they comfort me. — Psalms 23:4

Battle 2: Joshua 6:1-16

The Lord told Joshua that He was delivering the city of Jericho into his hands; the Lord also gave Joshua instructions on how to win the battle. They marched around the city as instructed. On the seventh day they marched around the city seven times, **the seven priests blew their trumpets, the people let out a loud shout unto the Lord, and then the walls of Jericho fell.**

Battle 3: Judges 7:1-22

Gideon's army numbered 300 and every solider in the army was given a trumpet. Gideon instructed all the troops to blow their trumpets at the same time along with him. The enemy ran, cried, and fled. The Lord set every man's sword against his fellow throughout the entire host. **The enemy, filled with fear, fled once the sound of praise went forth.**

Battle 4: 2 Kings 6:15-18

The enemy appeared to outnumber them, and Elisha prayed. *"Oh, my lord, what shall we do?" the servant asked.* The Lord opened the servant's eyes to see that a heavenly host with chariots of fire surrounded them. Then Elisha prayed that the enemy be struck with blindness. **Elisha, the prophet, who received the double portion of the anointing, prayed and the battle was won.**

Battle 5: 2 Chronicles 20:14-26

The battle of Jehosaphat was unique in that **singers and praisers were appointed to go before the army into combat.**

As they began to sing and praise the Lord, God came in suddenly and set ambushes against the enemy. Jehosaphat and all of Judah and Jerusalem knew how to worship the Lord. They also had to believe God's prophets so that they might prosper in this battle.

Summary of Winning Battles

Within each battle there were keys to victory, none of which ever appeared alone. There was always a combination of keys working together, such as praise and the word of God, instruments of praise and the word of God, faith and relationship, relationship and divine intervention, or faith and prayer. I have listed relationship as one of the primary keys to victory, which refers to a person having a personal relationship with Jesus Christ. The Word of God cultivates that relationship, bringing a deeper understanding of God's love, of His grace and mercy, and of His desire for good towards us. Out of that relationship, we can have faith to believe for deliverance, pray knowing that God will hear and respond, and speak well of God and praise Him from our heart. How can a person speak well of someone they don't really know? For praise to be effective as a spiritual weapon of warfare, there must be relationship.

Jesus, our Commander in Chief, knows the formation that His army must take in this hour in order to win the battle. We are receiving marching orders to praise the Lord. It is time for the army of God to arise armed with its spiritual weapons of warfare and instruments of praise. This army will not be silent, but declare the Word of the Lord. In unison this army will use their God given instruments of praise to create mighty sounds with their voices, hands, feet, and entire bodies along with all of the man made instruments. The prince of this world will be suffocated because of the radiant energy of praise filling the air. The enemy will shake at his knees in panic and terror, fleeing from us while his strongholds lose grip. What a victorious and overcoming army!

An Example of Warfare Praise Dance

The Spirit of God may reveal to you specific strongholds or demonic spirits that are attacking a ministry, person, or city. You can stand in the gap through prayer and through warfare and praise dance. First, begin by pulling down those strongholds, making the motions with you hands, reaching up, and pulling down. You can press them down or push them out with similar hand movements. Take dominion by treading with your feet, declaring that the ministry, person, or city belongs to the Lord. You can add props to enhance your movements. You might dance with a piece of red fabric to represent the blood of Jesus. Take a crown in your hand and dance with it to declare that Jesus is King and Lord over the ministry, person, or city. Dance until you feel peace about the situation. Then end the dance with leaps and turns of joy to proclaim that the victory is won.

I have personally experienced warfare dance to be the most intense when I'm in intercessory prayer at home, praying for a loved one. If I sense that a spirit is trying to attack that loved one, I will take my prayer into motion. While praying aloud, I begin carrying out forceful movements with my hands and feet. These actions are continued until I feel peace within my spirit. *"Dance is a powerful tool designed to affect the overall outcome of the power and authority God has entrusted to His people for spiritual warfare. I pray that we as the Church by the grace of God will come into the true understanding and function of dance in spiritual warfare."* [6]

Prophetic dance is another form of dance that can bring freedom and encouragement, but it is administered through the gift of prophecy.

The prince of this world will be suffocated because of the radiant energy of praise filling the air.

Warfare Dance

Now that we are familiar with some war terminology, let's explore ways to apply it to our dance. Warfare dance is one of the methods described in the "Technical Methods for the Ministry of Dance" chapter. Warfare dance is closely related to prophetic dance since both require sensitivity to the leading of the Holy Spirit. Warfare dance may also be referred to as warfare praise or warfare worship. Through warfare praise our entire bodies act out certain terminology mentioned in the scriptures implying war. For example, as we read Malachi 4:3, we are taught to tread down the enemy with the soles of our feet. One can make different movements with his feet to imply treading. We can actually praise ourselves or someone else right into victory. *"Warfare dance can be used at home to win territory for your loved ones, community, business, school system, and government in your community, or to intercede for the nation."*[5] Listed below are various terms of movement that can be incorporated into warfare dance.

Movement	Definition	Scripture
Arise	*quem*, get up, lift, hold up, stir, stand, strengthen	Micah 4:13
Beat with feet	*daqaq*, to crush, beat in small pieces, bruise, make into dust, make into powder, to stamp small	Malachi 4:3 Psalm 91:13
Bind	*deo*, to bind, be in bonds, knit, tie, wind	Matthew 16:19
Loose	*luo*, to loosen, breakup, destroy, dissolve unloose, melt, put off	Matthew 16:19
Pull Down	*Yarad*, to bring down, to cast down, subdue, take down	Proverbs 21:22
Push Down	*nagach*, to but with horns, to war against, gore, pushing down	Psalm 44:5
Seize	*Yarash,* to take, possession, cast out, destroy, drive out, expel	Joshua 8:7
Trample	*ramac*, to tread upon in walking, trample under feet, tread down	Psalm 91:13 Luke 10:19
Tread	*acac*, to trample, tread down	Joshua 1:3 Psalm 91:13 Malachi 4:3

5: Prophecy And Prophetic Dance

And afterward, I will pour out my Spirit on all people. Your sons and daughters will prophesy, your old men will dream dreams, your young men will see visions.

— Joel 2:28

We are so blessed to be living in a time and season when God is pouring out His Spirit on all people so that they might prophesy, dream dreams, and see visions. We live in a prophetic time and as we are sensitive to God's Spirit, we will be used to prophesy to others the Word of the Lord.

You may ask, what is prophecy? The Vine's Expository Dictionary states that prophecy is "the declaration of that which cannot be known by natural means, it is the forth-telling of the will of God whether with reference to the past, the present, or the future."[1]

The Office of a Prophet

A Prophet is one who speaks forth and proclaims a divine message from God. A prophet is also referred to as a seer, because he speaks in future tense and sees into the future as God reveals it to them. The prophet is one of the five-fold office gifts appointed to the church in order to equip and mature the saints for the working of the ministry.[3] God appoints a person to these offices, not man. Man can appoint those whom God has already called and appointed. The church is built on Apostles and Prophets as stated in Ephesians 2:20.

Consequently, you are no longer foreigners and aliens, but fellow citizens with God's people and members of God's household, built on the foundation of the apostles and prophets, with Christ Jesus himself as the chief cornerstone. In him the whole building is joined together and rises to become a holy temple in the Lord. And in him you too are being built together to become a dwelling in which God lives by his Spirit. — Ephesians 2:19-22

As we study the scriptures we find that prophets bring warning, correction, they tear down, they build up, they uproot, and they plant. They also comfort and encourage just as the gift of prophecy does. A prophet is one who speaks for God (Isa. 6:7-9). A prophet is one who sees (a seer) and is a watchman (Ezek. 3:17). The prophets of the Old Testament inquired of God for insight, guidance, counsel, and wisdom to instruct the people of God. God always reveals His plans to the prophets as stated in Amos 3:7.

To move in the prophetic dance in an orderly fashion, it is helpful for the person or persons involved in the dance to know and understand prophecy. If a person does not normally move in the prophetic realm outside of the dance ministry, he or she will not properly be able to dance and prophesy at the same time. When the Holy Spirit calls us to do something, He equips us to do it. That is why we are instructed to "study to show ourselves approved." God does not want "cornflake" Christians representing Him and bringing dishonor to His name. That does not mean that we cannot make mistakes. Peter made mistakes at times and yet God still said to him, "Feed my sheep." We need to understand that in all we do for and through God, we must have a servant's heart and a teachable spirit. We will be called wise, as in Proverbs, if we have a teachable spirit. We will be fools if we do not allow those over us to bring the necessary correction to our lives.[2]

— Dr. Aimee Verduzco Kovacs

Surely the Sovereign LORD does nothing without revealing his plan to his servants the prophets. — Amos 3:7

The Old Testament is filled with prophets and many of the Old Testament books are named after prophets. The prophet has a significant role in the lives of God's people and of the nation. Some of the New Testament Prophets were Agabus (Acts 21), Barnabus, and Symeon (Acts 13). A *prophetess* is a female prophet. Some of the prophetesses in the Old and New Testament were Miriam (Exod. 15), Deborah (Judg. 4), Noadiah (Neh. 6), and Anna (Luke 2).

The Gift of Prophecy

Not all of us are called to the office of the prophet; just as not all of us are called to be pastors, but we can all be prophetic people.[5] The Apostle Paul said in 1 Corinthians 14:39, "desire earnestly to prophesy, and do not forbid to speak with tongues." The gift of prophecy is one of the nine gifts of the Spirit outlined in 1 Corinthians 12. You can divide the gifts into three groups.

- *revelation gifts*: word of knowledge, wisdom, discernment of spirits
- *vocal gifts*: prophecy, different kinds of tongues, interpretation of tongues
- *power gifts*: working of miracles, faith, healings

The gift of prophecy is used to exhort, edify and to comfort. To exhort means to admonish, to urge one to pursue some course of conduct. To exhort is to build, to strengthen, and to bring encouragement. We all need to be encouraged at times. To edify means to build, therefore in a spiritual sense as we edify someone through prophecy, we are promoting spiritual growth and development in that person. Most importantly, as we minister in prophecy, we must do it in "love." I Corinthians 13:2 states that we can operate in many gifts, but without love, God sees them as noise, as a tinkling cymbal.

> **Prophetic Ministers are all other** ministers who do not have the office of the "prophet" but who do hold another office of the five-fold ministry and believe that there are prophets in the Church today. They may move in the prophetic ministry by prophesying with the gift of prophecy, or be giving personal prophecy with a prophetic presbytery, do prophetic counseling and ministry with gifts of the Holy Spirit, or minister in prophetic worship. All five-fold New Testament ministers in whichever office should be able to speak a rhema word revealing the mind and purpose of God for specific situations and people (2 Cor. 3:6, 1 Cor. 14:31).[4]
> — Dr. Bill Hamon

The topic of "love" takes us back to the chapter on "The Character of Christ" and growing in the fruit of the Spirit. God is more interested in our character rather than our spiritual gift.

In Acts 21:8 we read about Phillip the evangelist and his four daughters who had the gift of prophecy. Phillip's entire household flowed in the gift of prophecy. I believe that it is God's desire for His entire body to flow in the gift of prophecy. There is a great benefit in knowing and recognizing God's voice, so that we can receive His insight.

Prophetic Dreams, Visions and Interpretation

God spoke to the prophets and kings of the Old Testament in symbolic fashion, which required interpretation. An interpretation is simply an explanation of what is being said or done. Interpretation usually yields understanding. God often spoke in prophetic dreams or visions to give warning and instructions to the kings. Prophetic dreams and visions can be literal, but based on my personal experiences and the examples in the Bible they are usually symbolic. These dreams contained symbols or types, and without the interpretation, there would be no understanding. God usually speaks to us in this fashion so that we seek Him and search out the meaning and gain understanding. Proverbs 25:2 states that "*it is the glory of God to conceal a thing, but the glory of kings is to search out a thing.*" God conceals the meaning of the dream or vision within the symbols and types, but we are to search and seek for understanding. We can do this by first writing down the dream or vision. Next, we can highlight those things that are symbolic, such as objects, colors, words, or numbers, and then search out the meaning of the symbols through the scriptures. Most of all, we are to pray for the interpretation. God is the giver of the dream or vision, and only He can reveal the interpretation. Don't become discouraged if you don't get the full interpretation all at once. It may take days, weeks, months, or even years to get the full interpretation and understanding of what God is saying. It is important to write down the interpretation as you receive it so that you can refer back to it. You will eventually see the full picture of what God was painting for you through that dream or vision.

Let's take a look at what happened to King Nebuchadnezzar in the book of Daniel chapter two. The king was troubled in his spirit because of some dreams he had and could not remember them, but he wanted to know their meaning. Many of us have probably had an experience similar to the king's where we had a dream and could not remember the dream, but our spirit was troubled to know the dream and the interpretation. The king could not rest. He commanded that the magicians, astrologers, sorcerers, and Chaldeans come, show the king his dream, and interpret it. They soon found out that they could not meet the challenge. Daniel who knew God and had an intimate relationship with God could inquire of the Lord on such a matter and get results. Daniel inquired of God to know the king's dreams and they were revealed to Daniel in a night vision. Daniel blessed God for having all might, all wisdom, and all power to reveal the deep and secret things that are hidden from man. Daniel also thanked and praised God for the revelation and interpretation. Daniel then went before the king to tell him his dream and to interpret it. In verse 28, Daniel made this statement to the King, *"but there is a God in heaven who reveals mysteries. He has shown King Nebuchadnezzar what will happen in days to come."*

You may ask, "How do I know to which level of the prophetic God is calling me?" It is important not to overreact to your prophetic gifting and assume that you are called to the office of the prophet. God will affirm His prophets through others in the presbytery.

Parables and Spiritual Lessons

The prophets of old enacted their prophecies. One-third of the ministry of Ezekiel was in mime! Mime, drama, dance, and movement were all used in the delivery of the Word of God.

— Todd Farley

"A parable uses the objects of God's visible creation to teach us truths about His invisible and spiritual kingdom."[6] Jesus often taught in parables. These parables were stories or narratives that compared a natural experience to yield a spiritual lesson. The parables painted a picture of the message He was trying to convey. It is natural for our minds to formulate a picture whenever we hear or read a story. Many words in the Bible have symbolic meanings, such as colors, numbers, minerals, actions, directions, names and more. Whenever Jesus told a parable, many times He would next give the interpretation to bring understanding. There are close to forty parables that Jesus taught, not counting the ones that are repeated in several or all the Gospels. Jesus truly makes the phrase "a picture is worth a thousand words" come to life.

Several Old Testament prophets, Isaiah, Jeremiah, and Ezekiel, used parables. Isaiah 5:1-7 is a parable about a vineyard that yields wild grapes. This parable is speaking of Israel. Prophet Jeremiah heard the word of the Lord and obeyed by performing the actions as he was instructed. In Jeremiah 13:1-11, Jeremiah used *prophetic gestures* that declared what God was saying concerning Judah and Jerusalem. First, Jeremiah was instructed to purchase a linen girdle and tie it around his loins or waist. He was told not to wet it with water. Next, Jeremiah was told to arise, take the girdle, and hide it in a rock near the Euphrates River. Days later the Lord instructed Jeremiah to go dig up the girdle, when he did he saw that the girdle had decayed. The Lord said, *"After this manner will I mar the pride of Judah and the great pride of Jerusalem."* Just as the girdle clung to the loins of Jeremiah, God said He would cause the house of Israel and Judah to cling to Him that they might be His people, with a name, with praise, and with glory. The people chose not to listen or obey. The words that were spoken as a parable compared the experience of the girdle with what Judah and Jerusalem would experience. The prophetic gestures described in this text were the use of motions, objects, and the body as a means of expression. They were expressing an idea, sentiment, attitude, and emotion.

Prophetic Gestures

Gestures are movements and motions of the limbs or body as a means of expressing an emotion or intention. Through the use of prophetic gestures you are communicating a message with your movements while expressing a certain emotion or intention. Prophetic gestures are sometimes intertwined in the delivery of the message. "Jewish mime is seen when a prophet uses gestures and movements to communicate his message. These 'mimes' are delivered in three ways: 1) Actions with no narrative, 2) Actions with narrative before or after, 3) Actions with narrative given at the same time. Eighty percent of communication is non-verbal. This makes the message delivered with mime powerfully clear and very well communicated. The eight messengers who stand out in their use of mime are: Agabus, Ahijah, Angel in Revelation, Elisha, Ezekiel, Hosea, Isaiah, and Jeremiah."[7]

Prophet Agabus used both objects and gestures to convey a message from God. In Acts 21:10-12, Agabus took Paul's belt and bound it to his feet and hands. Agabus then spoke the words, *"This says the Lord. The Jews of Jerusalem shall bind like this the man who owns this belt and they shall deliver him into the hands of the Gentiles."* Objects along with the proper gestures or movements can help solidify the message.

The power of combining the gift of prophecy with movement gives you a visual demonstration. You are hearing and seeing it. You don't forget the picture image.

—

Deborah K. Smith

Movement	Interpretation	Scriptures
Bowing	humility, self-abasement, worship	Pss. 95:6; 145:14; 146:8; Rom. 11:4
Clapping	joy, victory, excitement	Pss. 47:1-2, 98:8
Dancing	joy, exuberance	2 Sam. 6:16; Ps. 30:11; Luke 15:25
Kneeling	worship, submission, surrender	Dan. 6:10; Mark 10:17; Acts 20:36
Lift Hands	praise, surrender, taking oath	Neh. 8:6; Ps. 14:12; 1 Tim. 2:8; Rev. 10:5
Running	zeal in the race of life	Heb. 12:1; Isa. 40:31; 1 Cor. 9:24-26
Standing	uprightness, standing one's guard	Luke 21:19; 1 Thess. 3:8; 1 Pet. 5:9
Walking	advancement, progress	Ps. 1:1-3; Isa. 2:3; 1 John 1:7

(Information from *Interpreting the Symbols and Types*[8])

All the discussion about the difference between the office of a prophet and the gift of prophesy, prophetic dreams, visions, interpretation, parables, prophetic gestures and symbolic movement brings us to *prophetic dance*. It is important to understand how the prophetic works in order to be able to effectively dance in the prophetic. Let's explore prophesying in the dance through prophetic dance.

Prophetic Dance

Prophetic dance, as we learned earlier, may be spontaneous or pre-planned (choreographed) and is Holy Spirit inspired. The dancer is lead by the Holy Spirit in his movements to deliver a particular message. The prophetic dancer operates in the gift of prophecy, but instead of the prophecy being spoken, it is danced.

Often a dancer may not know the exact message that God is speaking to the people, but the dancer must trust God to move through his movements prophetically and spontaneously. Sometimes the dancer will see the movements and then dance them out and may even use prophetic gestures as he dances. A dancer may dance prophetically with or without music, to instrumental music, or to music with lyrics. Instrumental music makes it easier for the dancer to focus on listening to what God is saying rather than interpreting the words of a song.

I have personally experienced the prophetic dance on several different levels. First, all praise goes to God for His awesome Spirit and anointing. God through His wonderful grace allows me to dance and to minister to His people under His anointing. It was through interpretive dancing that I first experienced being used prophetically. Many times God would place a song in my heart, and the movements in the dance and the gestures of my face and body would interpret the words of the song clearly for the people. Some of the people would respond as if they had just received a personal word from the Lord. I was invited, on one occasion, to dance in a historical program on a college campus. There were present some from the local government and many from the local middle and high schools. At the end of the program, a gentleman approached me with excitement in his voice. He said, pointing to the students in the bleachers, that he was an interpreter for the deaf students there that day. He continued saying that as I danced, he sat down and allowed the students to watch me because my dance interpreted the words of the song so beautifully. He could tell by the students' response they understood. Those comments from the interpreter blessed me deeply. Those students did not have the benefit of hearing the words of the song or the music, but their hearts were ministered to because the interpretive dance was clear. Interpretive dance paints a picture of the words being sung.

Interpretive dance can incorporate different styles or forms of dance while at the same time tell a story, preach a word, paint a picture, or literally speak the words of the song being played as the dance goes forth. Many times sign language is incorporated with this form of dance to add emphasis, meaning, or add drama. I personally feel that interpretive dance is the closest form of dance to prophetic dance. Interpretive dance is usually choreographed to the words of a song, and the prophetic dance is more spontaneous.

During the time when my husband and I were pastors of a small church, God placed a song in my heart while preparing for the Sunday service. He then told me to gather several objects and place them in a basket. That is all He told me, so I had to wait for further instructions. In the basket I had butterflies made of paper, candles, a red rose, a little bird, sunflower perfume, and some other small objects. I wasn't sure what it all meant, but I knew I had to wait until the next morning to see how things would unfold. During the morning worship, I danced and used each object to minister. As the song played, I took one object at a time and danced it around and before an individual. Nothing had been planned, I just picked up an object and went to the person I felt it was for and danced to the song. This was done for each individual present. The dance turned out to be a great blessing to each person. After the service I began to see how each object was prophetic for that given individual. God was letting the people know who they were in His eyes.

Spontaneous Prophetic Dance

I experienced prophetic dance on a completely new level while attending a prophetic conference. The prophetic atmosphere was ripe for anything to happen. Worship was intense as a guest psalmist sang the prophetic song of the Lord. The music flowed well and complimented the songs of worship. The presence of the Lord was almost tangible. As I stood at my seat in the pews, the anointing of God came upon me very strong. My hands felt like they were on fire. My arms flew up in the air and I began to dance at my seat. I couldn't shake it, and I was so overwhelmed that I screamed out while shaking my hands. The prophet of the house came over to me and took my hands and led me up to the stage area of the church. There I danced spontaneously and prophetically for over an hour. The music played and I danced. The psalmist sang and I danced. I can still remember that moment so vividly. After everything was over, I just laid in His presence. People later came up to me telling me how much the dance ministered to them.

Many times when the Lord and I are having our intimate times, I will dance before Him while at the same time relaxing my limbs (hands, arms, legs, and feet) to see what movements will come. In doing this God has given me new movements.

Prophetic Ministry and the Dance Team

I have always had a tug in my heart toward the prophetic gift and prophetic ministry. I longed to prophesy, because I had experienced the personal effects of a true word from God. I was blessed and I longed to bless others in the same way, desiring to comfort them in the same manner that I had been comforted. Through the positive experiences and good exposure to the prophetic early in my Christian walk, I have learned that a true word in season brings hope, joy, peace, and strength to go forward. Some people draw back from the prophetic because of negative past experiences. If you have had negative experiences with the prophetic ministry, trust God to heal you, forgive, and then step out in faith in this area again. Equip yourself with the Word of God as your anchor. God can use prophecy to bless you and others.

Some may hesitate to step out and prophesy because of fear of error. I would say to you pray, step out in faith, and minister in love. The thing that God gives you to share could be the very thing that will bring breakthrough, emotional healing, or confirmation to that person. Become a conduit for God so His message can go forth. We all ask God to use us, but when it comes to Him using us in the prophetic, we tend to withdraw. Open your heart and become a willing vessel.

1 Thessalonians 5:19-21 tells us not to quench the Spirit, nor despise prophesying, but to prove all things, holding fast to what is good. For those who are ministering, we are encouraged to allow the Spirit of God to flow and not quench the Spirit. For those who are receiving, we are encouraged not to look down on prophesy with contempt, but to test and examine that which is prophesied to us and to hold fast to that which is good. This scripture lays out some

boundaries in receiving prophecy. We all have been given a gift and we are to use it to serve others as stated in I Peter 4:10. If we are to speak (prophesy), we should do it as one speaking the oracles of God. As we dance prophetically, we must do it believing that God is speaking through our movements and gestures.

There are a few important things to remember before incorporating prophetic dance into the dance ministry. As emphasized before, an understanding of the prophetic is crucial. God will confirm His word through the scriptures, through our leaders, or through other prophetic people in our lives. He also confirms His word through dreams and visions. Several years ago, a night vision came to me of two motorcycles being pushed out. In the dream, I saw the dance team leader and myself on one motorcycle together. She straddled the end of the seat of the motorcycle while I sat closer to the front sitting side ways with both legs draped to one side. I was wearing a long flowing dress. The driver was a male form but I did not see his face. Sitting between the other dance leader and me seemed to be small children. There were a total of five on the one motorcycle including the driver. The ride was not completely smooth at first, and the bike was slightly weaving from side to side. The dance leader yelled, "Hey, what's going on up there?" She then proceeded to ask me to drape my legs over to the other side of the bike. After I made that adjustment, the ride became smooth. I fell asleep during the ride and wondered, why it was that I did not fall off during the ride. The dream shifted to another scene where I was laying hands on a lady's head and prophesying to her.

I learned at a prophetic conference hosted in Charlotte, N.C., that a motorcycle usually represents the prophetic ministry.[8] When I awoke from the dream, I knew that the dream was about the prophetic. The two motorcycles represented two individuals being pushed out into prophetic ministry. I also recognized some of the other symbols in the dream. The two of us riding on the same motorcycle could mean that we both have the same

When you have not a clue, continue to do.

type of anointing or ministry or that God was going to use us together in the prophetic ministry. Since we are members of the same dance team, it could represent a prophetic dance ministry that God desires to advance. The dance leader in the dream is the dance leader of our church dance team. I believe the dress represented an anointing as well as the dance ministry. My legs being shifted from the right side to the left showed us moving forward more smoothly as we depend on God's strength and not our own strength. The sleeping part of the dream made me nervous until I understood the meaning. The sleeping represented us sleeping on the ministry in which God wants us to move. God doesn't want us unaware or unconscious of where we are and where He wants to take us.

The Prophetic Minister

During a prophetic dance session, the speaker, Dr. Abigail Mobely, shared some points about the prophetic minister. I share them along with my personal thoughts.

Must Have and Must Do

- Be willing to die to self and allow God to increase in order to minister a dance to an individual or congregation.
- Have a love relationship with Christ, with the Word so that the anointing of God will flow.
- Have a sincere heart and a genuine concern for others to see them blessed by God.
- Yield your members to God and follow His leading.
- Do not fight or quench the Spirit, but flow with the leading of the Holy Spirit
- Have the attitude, "Not my will, but thy will be done."
- Walk a life of obedience to God, to His Word, and be a worshiper.
- Be a student of God's Word and study the Word on a frequent basis.
- Prophesy in unconditional love.
- Be a willing and available vessel for God.
- Become comfortable with being uncomfortable. The prophetic is operated by faith and through obedience.
- Walk in submission to authority and leadership.

- Practice entering God's presence during personal prayer and worship time; this makes it easier to enter in during a corporate setting.
- Build dance technique and skill.
- Give God the glory.
- Pray against the spirit of pride.

Prophetic Dance Training and Activation

One evening while preparing to teach a prophetic dance class, I struggled before the Lord with the question, "How can we make this class less intimidating for students?" This was my first time teaching this particular group of students and I had no clue if they had even heard of prophetic dance. Prophetic dance is often intimidating for those who have not seen and experienced it, especially to those who are new to this form of dance. Then I heard within my spirit, train them to prophesy in the dance, prophesy and interpret.

I interceded for the students and asked God for prophetic words to minister in the dance. God knew the students and He knew who would be there that night; therefore, He knew what prophetic words to give me to write down. Afterwards, I had eight prophecies to share with the class. I then typed the prophecies making a copy of each. On one copy I typed the word "prophesy" and on the other copy I typed "interpret." I then added key words and tips to the "prophesy" sheet.

During the class, after teaching a scriptural foundation about the prophetic, I proceeded to hand out the slips of paper. Some students received a slip of paper with "prophesy" on it and the others received a slip of paper with "interpret" on it. I placed objects, fabrics, and props around the room to be used during the prophetic dance. I explained that each person had either a paper with "prophesy" or "interpret" and that after completing her prophetic dance, the person who felt she was holding the interpretation would read the interpretation for everyone to hear. I then explained that the purpose of the key words and tips was to help them formulate movements based on those key words as well as to initiate the use of objects in their dance. A key word underlined signified that an object was available to use for the prophetic dance.

As a demonstration, I danced out the first prophecy. During

the dance, I went to the person that I felt the prophetic word was for and presented the person the object that I used during the dance. After I finished the dance, I asked who was holding the interpretation in their hand. The person holding the interpretation then read it aloud. This process continued until all the prophetic words had been danced and interpreted. Each prophetic dance matched exactly with the correct interpretation. It was amazing! Tears flowed as each person was ministered to, and God's anointing blessed everyone present. I witnessed each person flowing in a new level of freedom. Having the prophetic word in their hands helped build their confidence to dance prophetically. I had several students tell me that they had experienced prophetic dance before, but this was a much less intimidating approach.

> **The unique thing about the dancing** women in 1 Samuel 18:6-8, is that they were prophesying <u>while they were dancing</u> about something that was going to happen. Note: David had not killed his "ten thousands" yet, but he surely would.[9] — Deborah K. Smith

Personal Prophetic Ministry

The hearts of the people are longing to hear from God. They are longing for spiritual direction and encouragement. Thank God for the gift of prophecy! God has placed the gift of prophecy in our reach to encourage, comfort, strengthen, and instruct others. There is another level of prophetic dance ministry that is more personal. Just as there is corporate prophecy or a word for the church, there is also personal prophecy, a word for an individual. The examples that I shared earlier were all done before a group of people or before a congregation. That was more like corporate prophecy. The dances were ministered unto the Lord and unto the people as a whole.

We can also do personal prophecy in the dance. Instead of speaking what is seen or heard, it is danced before the person receiving ministry. Stepping out into the prophetic takes faith and confidence in God. You may only hear in your thoughts or spirit the word "joy" then you will dance out "joy" in whatever way God gives it to you to express. As you step out in faith, more words may come. Dance them out as well, while trusting the Holy Spirit as your helper.

I danced around a young lady during a prophetic dance session. The first movements were very precise ballet movements. Next, I transitioned to bending movements with my arms stretched forward. The last movements were leaping, running, and dancing in freedom. The dance prophesied to her, saying that she no longer had to dance in her own strength. That God had or was bringing freedom and liberty in her dance that would bring her much joy. After I finished the dance, someone interpreted and the words confirmed the movements that were prophesied in the dance. The young lady, filled with joy, stood there in tears.

Key Things to Remember Before Starting Personal Prophetic Dance Ministry Time

- Always pray as a group, asking God to take charge and to have His way during your time together.
- Pray for God to release His prophetic anointing so that you all may prophesy.
- Give all your cares and burdens over to God and focus on Him.
- Don't be afraid to step out and dance what you see, hear, sense, or feel.
- Remember that personal prophecy is to exhort, edify, or to comfort, to bring encouragement in love.
- God will use your five senses many times to speak to you.

Ways That God May Speak to You

- Vision – You may see a picture in your mind
- Thought – You may think or hear a word or words
- Emotion – You may feel a certain emotion
- Scripture – A scripture may come to your mind
- Smell – You may smell a certain fragrance in your nostrils
- Touch – You may touch a person and discern more or God gives you more specifics

Group Exercises for the Dance Team

A. Play a portion of a song and have the dancers write down what they see, hear, or feel. Also, have them write down the key words that they hear and can express in movement. Next, have each person share from his writings. Play the song again and have each person dance the words that he wrote.

B. After prayer, read I Corinthians 14:3 which states the purpose of the gift of prophecy.

  - Explain that you are about to have personal prophetic ministry time and that they will dance instead of speak.
  - Place your group in a circle formation.
  - Pick one person to be the receiver and place that person in the center of the circle. Have different individuals that want to prophesy go before the person and dance out what they see, hear, feel, or think. If a person wants to use a prop such as a cloth, flag, Bible, praise hoop, or streamer, encourage him to do so.
  - Then select another individual to be the receiver and continue the activity as time permits.

It is always good to have facial tissues available because tears flow when the Spirit of God moves and touches hearts through personal prophetic ministry. Personal prophetic ministry is healthy for your dance team because individuals are being encouraged, while learning how to minister to others on a personal level. Cherish those personal prophetic ministry times, for the dance team usually focuses on ministering to God and to others corporately and not to each other.

Creating an Atmosphere for the Prophetic

During the corporate setting of praise and worship, the musicians and song leaders can use their instruments to help establish a prophetic atmosphere. Instruments produce music and the music becomes a catalyst for the prophetic. Whenever a musician plays music inspired by the Holy Spirit that inspiration in itself is prophetic. The prophetic is also already in operation when a psalmist sings a new song unto the Lord. A person that is easily inspired by the Holy Spirit to play can accompany a dancer as he ministers in the prophetic. This is an awesome combination. If you add the prophetic song along with the music and dance, who knows what God may do in your midst.

The prophet Samuel anointed Saul in accordance to God's call and direction. Samuel then proceeded to give Saul instructions from God. Samuel told Saul that he would go to the city of Gibeah and there he would meet a procession of prophets coming down from the high place prophesying. An interesting thing to note about this passage is that there were instruments being played before the prophets as they prophesied. Here you see worship and the prophetic together. The music provided an atmosphere for the prophetic to flourish. Samuel also told Saul that the Spirit of the Lord would come upon him in power and he would prophesy. The atmosphere was filled with the prophetic, the spirit of prophecy was present, and Saul began to prophesy like the prophets. 1 Samuel 10:5-12 tell us that the musicians and dancers were marching before the processional of prophets. There were lyres, tambourines, flutes, and harps being played. I personally believe that there were dancers carrying those tambourines, making a joyful noise unto the Lord. Many times when the word tambourine is mentioned in the Bible it is in conjunction with dancing. [10]

> I will build you up again and you will be rebuilt, O Virgin Israel. Again you will take up your tambourines and go out to dance with the joyful. — Jeremiah 31:4

> In front are the singers, after them the musicians; with them are the maidens playing tambourines.
> — Psalm 68:25

Asaph, one of the Old Testament prophets referred to as a seer was also a minstrel of music. Asaph and his associates were before the ark of the covenant of the Lord to minister regularly. Some of the sons of Asaph were set apart for the ministry of prophesying, accompanied by harps, lyres, and cymbals. They were appointed to those positions, but were under the supervision of their father, a prophet who prophesied under the King's supervision. Asaph submitted to the Kings' authority, and his sons submitted to his authority (1 Chron. 25: 1-3). Submission is another key factor to your growth and development in the ministry. You must be submissive to the leadership within the church. As the sons of Asaph submitted to their father, he could then help groom them and perfect their prophetic gifts.

Likewise, even if your pastor knows nothing about the prophetic or prophesying, your submission to leadership will cause you to gain favor, and the Lord will bless you. Don't give up. If the ministry or church in which you are a member does not embrace the ministry of the prophetic or is not yet ready for it yet, pray. It may be a vision that God has for that particular ministry or church, but you must allow God to prepare the hearts of the people in His time. Use your private times with God to expand yourself in spontaneous worship.

My prayer is that you go forth in the prophetic dance and in the gift of prophecy for the fulfillment of scripture "that all may prophesy." Enjoy the process as God carries you from glory to glory.

When God Clues You In

Deborah Smith is the dance team leader of Vessels of Honor at Harvest Cathedral Church. During their dance conferences, Deborah conducts prophetic dance sessions. The sessions begin with prayer followed by a short teaching. Deborah then states the assignment and the prophetic ministry begins among the students. Through the prophetic dance we have seen God minister incredibly, bringing confirmation, encouragement, and hope. There is always a giver and a receiver in prophecy. In some assignments, the dancers are paired off to minister one to one. A dancer prophesies in the dance while the other receives ministry. Each person is asked to switch roles so that both will have the opportunity to minister and to receive. Following is an example of one of the activation sessions.

Two ladies were selected randomly and called to the stage to demonstrate prophetic dance. These ladies had never met before and knew absolutely nothing about each other. One lady began to dance around the other lady. The dancer began to make movements that resembled something like a flower coming out of the ground evolving into life. A psalmist played music as the dance unfolded. The psalmist began to sing a song prophetically putting words to the movements. Everyone now could see and hear the message being conveyed. "Out of death and burial God is going to bring forth life," were the words that flowed. The dancer who was receiving ministry just began to sob. Once the song and dance ended, Deborah asked the ladies to share. The dancer that demonstrated the movement then shared that she was divorced and asked the other dancer if she was divorced or separated from her spouse. The lady replied that she and her husband had been separated for quite a while, but the dance confirmed to her that God was going to resurrect their relationship and their marriage would be restored. The dancer began her movements by faith, and then God began to clue her in on the message that He was speaking to the other dancer. The message was also confirmed through prophetic song. This was an amazing experience for everyone present.

Helpful Hint

In order to flow in prophetic dance, one must become comfortable in dance and put his total focus on God while freely praising Him. Have faith in God's ability to minister through you. Then just dance whatever comes to you. Your body may sometimes make the movements before your mind can even see the movements.

6: Teaching Your Fingers To War
Signing and Dance

How might we enhance our movements in the ministry of dance by applying some of the methods that were described? We can do this by layering. We can combine those methods, or we can add things to increase visual communication. This can be done in several ways. We can incorporate sign language into our dance choreography.

Signing is one of the many formal languages spoken in the United States and in countries all around the world. We can use our hands to speak to others and to speak to God. I believe that sign language is being brought forth in the church for two reasons: one to evangelize the deaf community, and second to incorporate the language in the performing arts ministry. Signing is becoming an art in the 21st century. Many ministries are forming sign teams as a part of their worship service. A team or an individual can sign an entire song while the music and the words of the song are being played.

Signing within dance is absolutely beautiful. The gestures done with the hands add so much more to a dance. Signing can be used in expressive worship and interpretive dance. When we dance, we speak from our heart and with our body language. Signing can take that communication to a whole new level. Silent words of praise are going before the throne and into the ear of God. Those silent words may be speaking to someone present who is naturally deaf. If ministry does occur, those silent words can induce silent tears as God speaks to their heart. We must be careful as we choreograph a dance incorporating sign language to use the sign correctly and clearly when ministering in the dance. When using the hand gestures in dance, it is not necessary to sign every word spoken within the song. We can choose key words of a song to sign to help the dance flow. Strictly signing is upper body movement only, but dance that blends in signing is movement of the entire body.

I encourage the congregation to learn sign or at least some key words used in praise and worship songs so that they can join in signing while a song is being sung. Becoming more of a participator rather than a spectator will take individual praise and worship to a whole new glorious level. We are actually speaking to God in a known language.

At times satan will come and bring thoughts to try and discourage us from praising God, especially during congregational worship. We may hear thoughts like, 'you are just trying to be seen', or 'you are just raising your hands and dancing for show.' The enemy will tell us that everyone is watching and that we look foolish. As those thoughts come, we must pull down every imagination and stronghold by lifting our hands higher and dancing on the devil's head even more. We must remember that God has called us first to be worshipers of Him. God is pleased to see our focus is on Him and Him alone. As we continue to stand against the thoughts of the devil, we become even freer within our worship and praise unto God. At the same time, we will be embarking upon new territory in spiritual warfare and clearing the airways for others to become free from the very same thoughts. Praise is a wonderful way to combat the enemy. We can teach our fingers to war through the art of signing.

I recommend that you purchase a sign book for your personal library. You can also go to your local public library to check out a book on signing. Choose a song, and begin to practice using the some of the signs found in the book.

Becoming more of a participator rather than a spectator will take individual praise and worship to a whole new glorious level.

Helpful Hint

Cast down vain imaginations!

The enemy will try to discourage you to keep

you from praising the Lord.

"Resist him" (1 Pet. 5:9).

PRACTICAL ELEMENTS

1: Organizing A Dance Team

The remainder of this book is a compilation of those things that are more practical to the workings of a dance ministry. Many people ask the question, "How do you get started?" To whom do you go and what do you do? You may be in the same position that I was in about twelve years ago. Your Pastor has asked you to start a dance ministry and organize a dance team in your church.

The pastor desires to broaden the outreach of the church by coordinating and utilizing the performing arts, and more specifically the dance in order to minister and evangelize. You are excited within your spirit, but shaking at the knees because you haven't a clue as to what to do. You may be one whom God has placed a specific vision for the dance ministry in your heart and you approach the pastor with the details seeking approval. Regardless of how we each start out, we all end up at the same point, by asking God for divine insight, guidance, and direction.

It was a major milestone in my life when my former pastor approached me with this marvelous idea of starting a dance team. Just to give you a little background on how it all started, one afternoon after church service a few ladies and I were discussing the details and plans for the pastor's birthday celebration dinner. They made mention of having seen a dance team perform at some other event and expressed an interest in having someone dance at the celebration. I shared that I was taught a Christian dance during my last year in college while attending a ministry located off campus. The ladies were quick to respond with excitement, "Would you dance at the pastor's birthday celebration dinner?" My mouth dropped open with dismay and I responded, "I can't do that because I've only danced once and

I don't even have a dance song." After their pleading and begging, I finally gathered up enough nerve to say yes. I prayed and asked God to give me a song to dance to, and one night God awakened me with the words of a song ringing in my mind along with the movements for a dance. I was so excited that I could hardly go back to sleep. God was faithful to give me a song and a dance. After dancing at the celebration, the pastor approached me with the question, "Will you start a dance team ministry in our church?" I was flabbergasted to say the least, but I responded with a yes while thinking that he would probably forget we ever had the conversation. Several weeks passed and the pastor approached me again asking a similar question, "When are you going to start the dance team?" I then told him that I would send out a letter to all of the ladies in the church to see who might be interested and then schedule a date for our first team meeting. God gave the vision for the ministry and it was history from that point on. The dance ministry grew from one person to two, then to six, and next into a full sacred arts ministry with three different age groups of dancers, a mime team, and a drill team. The dancers ministered in one form or another during each church service. Although I am at a new church now, that dance ministry is still flourishing today. I am thrilled to know that God has blessed in such an awesome way. I thank my former pastor for pushing me out into the deep and into a divine stream where God had destined me to flow.

My passion for the ministry of dance has grown to heights and depths that I never dreamed possible. God has developed me through interpretive dance, expressive worship and into prophetic dance. He has stretched me and continues to stretch me into a vessel fit for the Master's use. I am so glad that God matures and transforms us through His divine Word. He stretches us according to His divine plan for our lives. Regardless of where you are right now, God has a plan for your life. Through your faith and trust in Him you will see God go beyond that which you could ever imagine.

To answer the first two questions in this section, "To whom do you turn and what do you do?" first turn to God for guidance, and then to other available resources. I immediately began to build my resource library. When I first started, resources for the dance ministry were terribly limited, but God continues to expand His resource pool. Dance and other worship arts conferences are very helpful because you are able to make more contacts and establish variety for your dance team.

Become a student of the Word and study about dance, praise, and worship. Purchase books, audios, and videos referencing the dance in ministry and worship arts. Allow God to expand your territory in this area of your life. Begin to carry a notebook to write down different ideas, songs, or movements that you get, see, or hear. Sometimes if you don't write it down you will lose that thought and have to struggle to remember it later. Begin to build your music or song library as well. Prioritize time in your schedule to listen to worship or praise music and worship the Lord. During these times God will draw you to a particular song for the dance team. Listening to Christian radio stations will also help expand your knowledge of what songs are available.

Don't carry the burden of the ministry alone. Enlist others on the dance team to help. They could have their eyes and ears open for new resources, listen for songs to dance to, and even help with choreography. Also listen for the theme of the pastor's sermons or teaching series so that you will be more sensitive to songs carrying a similar message. You could actually choreograph a dance to complement the Word of God going forth to the people, and minister in dance just before the pastor gets up to speak. In that way the people will receive the Word visually and audibly.

Now that we have explored the answers to the questions, let's review some keys that are important for a successful dance team.

Keys for a Successful Dance Team

1. *Team Prayer*
   While in prayer, seek God to discover what He is saying and wants to communicate to the congregation. Pray for God to anoint the dance. Pray for Him to minister to and deliver His people. Pray that He will choreograph and organize the dance. Pray for unity among the dancers. During group prayer it is always good to pray for any immediate needs of the dancers and their families.

2. *Prepare for the Dance Ministry – A tri-fold preparation*
   • <u>Spiritual Readiness</u>: During the dance rehearsal prayer time there should be a time of searching and purifying motives, and an acknowledgment of any offense against another. If

someone offends you, ask God to help you to forgive him. God will give you further instructions if anything else is necessary, such as going to the person and talking to him about whatever happened and how it made you feel. If you know that you have offended someone, the Bible tells us to go make amends, to go that person and make things right. God wants your team to be spiritually and emotionally healthy.

- <u>Bible Study</u>: Grow in knowledge of God's Word. Study the scriptures concerning praise, worship, and dance. Seek the Lord while in the Word. He will give you instructions concerning such matters as holiness, love, repentance, unity, humility, faith, and others.

- <u>Rehearsal</u>: The dancer's body is the vehicle for worship. A dancer for God must become "a vessel that moves!" Times of spontaneity and creativity should be encouraged during rehearsal. The dancers must know that as they have submitted themselves to the will of God and committed themselves to the dance ministry, they have an obligation to maintain a consistent prayer life and be committed to weekly rehearsals or whatever frequency your team decides. Emphasize that the sanctuary is no place for performance, but for worship and for ministry.

During the times of congregational worship, dancers can participate with the congregation by worshipping in spontaneous joy of the Lord or in solemn reverence inspired by God. The dancers may be stationed at their seats or around the sanctuary praising the Lord. This time of worship is to inspire spontaneity and to release others around you to be free in their praise to God. This type of dancing is unplanned and is so liberating. It is almost like you are standing right in front of the throne of God.

Choreographed dance ministry time is usually staged and done before the congregation as a dance presentation. There may be other times when the dancers will join in with the worship team, dancing simple choreography for some of the worship songs.

Worship should become a part of every dancer's lifestyle. It is important to spend time worshipping God. I personally call it "practicing being in God's presence." This should be a part of our daily walk. We must discipline ourselves to make melody unto the Lord. Even in the demands of a busy day, our hearts should be filled with inward worship, thanksgiving, and adoration. That is not always an easy task, which is why it's considered a sacrifice. As stated earlier, praise and worship is more than dancing and singing. Praise and worship is extolling God for His mighty works as we declare His character and His ways with our words. The more we seek the Lord in our private time, the more sensitive we become in recognizing His presence during congregational worship. As worship becomes a lifestyle for us, the anointing of God will begin to flow out of our life. God will anoint us for ministry.

> The heart is deceitful above all things and beyond cure. Who can understand it? "I the LORD search the heart and examine the mind, to reward a man according to his conduct, according to what his deeds deserve." — Jeremiah 17:9-10

Praying with and for the Team

It is important that all members of a ministry team pray for that ministry as a group and individually. Prayer brings unity among the team. Whenever the team gathers to pray, touching and agreeing, making request unto God, He is there with them and hears the petitions. Team prayer invites God in to help with the rehearsals. He will be present to help with timing and order, with the choreography, or whatever the need is at that particular time and place. We can approach the throne of grace with confidence to receive help in our times of need. The Bible tells us to pray continually, without ceasing, knowing that the Father hears and answers prayers.

Many challenges will come within the ministry, but we must always pray and not give up. Throwing up our hands to give up is the easiest way out, but standing within the midst of uncertainty and praying for the vision when there appears to be "di-vision" is what God uses to make true God-fearing and anointed ministers and leaders. When there is division within the team, we cannot allow fear or anxiety to inhibit us.

The peace of God will come to encourage each of us as we pray about the situation. Try not to get too anxious when some of the team members are not cooperating, just bring them before the Lord in prayer. God will try their hearts, change them, or move them. As leaders, it is most essential that we seek the motive of our own heart in everything we do, especially when there is conflict. As we give God permission, He will examine our hearts. We must ask God to pinpoint the problem, to show whether it is within us or it is someone else. It is important that we always keep our hearts open to the Lord for correction. Let's welcome God into every area of our lives, so that His Spirit can function as a spotlight to keep our hearts and motives pure. The enemy would then have to look elsewhere for a weapon to use against us.

Team Transitions

Every team goes through different stages and transitions. Don't become weary of the task at hand. When a few people first gather together and say that they are a team, they're really not there yet. The team may have a name, but it takes time to become a "TEAM." Remember this: TEAM means Together Effectively Accomplishing Mission.

The dictionary states that a team is a number of persons associated together in work or activity, a group on one side being yoked or joined. It also states that teamwork is done by several associates with each doing a part, but all subordinating personal prominence to the efficiency of the whole.[1] Each individual submits himself and any personal agendas to the working of the team mission.

One of the first activities a group should do as a team is to prepare a vision or mission statement. In some cases the vision or mission statement may already exist for the dance ministry and may only need to be revised. The mission statement should state the purpose of the team and ministry. Develop a list of expectations so that everyone clearly knows what is expected as a team member. As a measure of alignment with the overall church vision, the delegated leader is responsible for sharing the vision and mission statement with the pastor.

Next, a list of team norms should be developed, such as the meeting time, meeting location, and the frequency your team will meet. It is always good to develop a quarterly calendar to list meeting dates and special activities. You can also keep track of each team member's birthday by the using the same calendar. The development of team roles and responsibilities may or may not be necessary. Team roles will vary from team to team. I have been a member of several teams; some had just the delegated leader, while others had several roles for the team. Some of the roles may include:

- Team, Ministry or Auxiliary Leader
- Team Leader Assistant(s)
- Garment or Dance Uniform Coordinator
- Props Coordinator
- Team Notebook Coordinator

TEAM means Together Effectively Accomplishing Mission

To avoid becoming overwhelmed, it is a good idea to start with the few essential roles and then add roles as needed. After all of the basics and foundational areas are set for the team, all the team information should be typed and distributed to each team member for future reference.

The Stages of Team Development

There are five stages of team development. Four are most commonly experienced among teams, and the fifth stage occurs from time to time over the life span of a team. These terms, Forming, Storming, Norming, Performing, and Transforming are used in the business world when referring to team transitions.[2] In this section I will list the characteristics of the person within each stage. I will also point out common tasks that are associated with each team development stage. The content has been modified to fit ministry teams.

Stage One: Forming

In this stage two or more individuals decide that they want to work toward a common goal. This stage is awkward due to the newness of the relationships among team members. This stage is characterized by polite attitudes; individuals have a need for acceptance, and a need for guidance and direction. Most of the topics discussed during this stage are serious or broad, where feelings are avoided. There is little "real" communication taking place among the team members, just surface talk. The members are usually impersonal, watchful, and guarded during the forming stage. Some may experience anxiety over roles, especially if leadership has not yet been established for the group. At times in this stage there are poor attempts to define the task, yielding a less desirable response of tentative involvement from team members.

Task for Team Development in Forming Stage
• Agree on common goals.   • Define the task and how it will be accomplished.   • Establish a base level of expectations and similarities.

As you transition from stage to stage, you will notice that each stage builds on the previous stage preparing for the performing (ministering) stage. Skipping any of the first three stages could ultimately have a negative affect in accomplishing your mission to minister.

Stage Two: Storming

In this stage the group strives to become a team. One person has his ideas about what the team should be doing and the other person is thinking something totally different. There may be a conflict in personalities, which can cause uneasiness for the team.

Sometimes people are unsure of each other's motives, which may also cause conflict. There may even be evidence of those ugly spirits of jealousy and competition, causing competitive jealousy to surface. Other negative characteristics are often evident in the storming stage such as arguments, increased tension, frustration, defensiveness, and taking everything personally. In this stage individuals try to find their place and try to fit in. If you are the leader, you should let everyone know that the things they are experiencing as a team are normal, and it too will pass as you transition while taking the proper steps to become more of a team. This is all a part of the Storming stage of teaming. Much prayer, communication, and teaching will begin to "calm the storm."

We must be cautious not to have a self-serving, what about me attitude. It is important to have a desire to grow, but our heart should be asking what can I do to serve and not what will I get for serving?

Task for Team Development in Storming Stage

- Learn about other members on the team. Spend time together outside of the normal team gatherings.
- Express differences in ideas, feelings, and opinions. You may even consider having a team notebook for recording ideas that the members express for the team. A person might have a really good idea, but the timing may be wrong.
- Gain skills in communication. Identify other resources such as the Bible and other books that assist in growth.
- There must be respect for the leader and a mutual respect for each team member. We are to apply the principle of treating others the way we desire to be treated.
- Deal with power and control issues. Calm the storm by addressing the issues and pray for wisdom and seek solutions through the Word.

I feel that it is important to address the spirit of competitive jealousy because of the great devastation it can bring to relationships and to the team's success. If there is competition on your team, take the matter to God first. "The words competitive and competition come from the root word to compete which simply means 'to seek or to strive for the same things as another, to carry on a contest or a rivalry for a common objective.' Competition, in and of itself, can be good or bad. Like anything else, it depends upon your perspective or context."[3] Many times the spirit of competition rears its ugly head whenever individuals are insecure in themselves. The spirits of jealousy or inferiority are close kin to the spirit of competition. Jealousy "is the sense of uneasiness or anxiety that stems from the fear of preference being given to another. Take the powerful drive of competitiveness, combine it with the volatile poison of jealousy and you have a lethal combination. Competitive jealousy is more than an emotion, it's a spirit. Competitive jealousy urges me to compare. Competitive jealousy drives me to compare myself with someone else. It always provokes me to compete for favor, for position, for power, for authority, for influence. Ultimately, the spirit of competitive jealousy will compel me to criticize others in order to make myself look better."[4]

Whenever one experiences an attack from the spirit of competition, be on the look out for one of the other cousins, because that spirit does not act alone. Someone may be there for the wrong reason, to perform and not to minister. Pray about the situation; ask God to search your heart continuously to keep yourself free. Begin to thank and praise God for everyone and their perfect place on the team. Continue to pray against the spirit of competitive jealousy so that there will be unity, and the anointing will flow.

Stage Three: Norming

We can all breathe a little easier now that we have transitioned into the Norming stage. This stage is characterized by positive attributes. The team members begin to experience a sense of cohesion and cooperativeness. In this stage there is more discussion of team dynamics and sharing of personal problems. When a difference of opinion arises, the ability to express disagreement and constructive criticism is evident. There is less emotional conflict and greater shared leadership.

As mentioned earlier, the development of the team vision and mission statement should be done before or soon after the team forms. The development of team norms such as ground rules, roles, and responsibilities are all a part of the Norming stage. When each member knows and understands the vision and mission of the team, linking that with taking ownership in a role or responsibility, they become more at ease. Everyone is now on common ground and working from the same page. The team agrees on norms and procedures for working together, which creates an atmosphere of respect, harmony, and feelings of mutual trust. A sense of closeness has been established. If the spirit of inferiority was the root cause to induce the spirit of competition, then by this stage of team development the competitive relationships should become more cooperative. People can now envision their contribution and significance to the team. The sense of feeling threatened should dissolve during this stage.

This is the time to ask each person on the team how he would like to contribute. One may be good at sewing and may want to contribute by working with team garments and props. One may have taken different forms of dance and may be able to help teach dance technique or work with the choreography of team dances. One may be an intercessor and can intercede for the dance ministry. One may enjoy working with crafts; this may be the person to make the team dance props, or one may want to assist in all of the areas. During this time team members begin to find their place and begin to function within that place.

Task for Team Development in Norming Stage
• Agree upon team norms, ground rules, roles and responsibilities. • Agree on processes for problem-solving. • Accept the individuality of each team member. (God has made us all unique).

Stage Four: Performing (with the Intent to Minister)

Collaboration occurs within the Performing stage. There is good understanding of members' strengths and weaknesses. Team members are more comfortable and self-assured. There is high group morale, trust, and loyalty with a genuine sense of caring about one another. Members feel a close attachment to the group, like being a part of a family unit.

In this stage there is more clarity of mission, goals, roles, responsibilities, and ministry expectations. There is involvement of all team members contributing to a cooperative and productive team climate. Open, relevant, and focused communication occurs within this stage.

There is a great amount of faith, commitment, and discipline required in becoming a highly effective ministering team. Teaching sessions should be scheduled from time to time to equip the team spiritually. Biblical teaching brings understanding of the ministry purpose. The teaching of godly character and the fruit of the spirit help to combat that spirit of competition. The team foundation and scriptural foundation is what takes a team over the performing level into the ministering level. It is essential that a ministry team adjoin itself with biblical teaching. Prayer will be like an adhesion, and the Word of God will launch the team forth to function as one unit, in one spirit. There will always be issues, but God will impart the strength and ability to deal with the issues as they come. Remember God equips those He calls and He will not put more on you than you can bear.

Whatever the mission is at hand, the team members will join together to accomplish the mission. Maybe your team is preparing for a special presentation on a church program and new praise enhancers are needed, the choreography must be developed for one or more songs, and a few of the dance garments have spots or unpleasant odors, then it is time for all team members to pull together. Some members may work on the props, while others choreograph dances. Then another may volunteer to wash the garments. Now, that's a team working together for ministry purpose.

Task for Team Development in Performing Stage
• Overall goal is to be effective in ministry.   • Achieve effective and satisfying solutions to problems.   • Roles and authority dynamics must adjust to the needs of the group.

Stage Five: Transforming

The transforming stage does not occur as frequently as the previous mentioned team development stages. It occurs from time to time over the course of the life of a team. Transforming occurs whenever a team is forced to deal with periods of significant change, such as a losing or adding team members, redefining the team's purpose, or totally restructuring the team. Whenever new team members are added to a team, the team will experience a period of transforming, which may even cause or force the team to revisit the earlier stages of teaming. For certain the new member will experience some of the feelings and emotions seen in the earlier stages of teaming. The new person may feel nervous or anxious while an older team member may feel threatened by the new member's presence or skill level.

Many times a team will experience transformation whenever leadership changes. If the new leader is not properly introduced and transitioned in well, the team may experience drastic changes causing it to "regress." The key is to begin again at step one in prayer, working your way through the development stages.

Task for Team Development in Transformation Stage
• Revisit the earlier stages of team development.   • The older members should encourage the new members.   • Rejoice at the opportunity for growth.

The dance team is like a woven piece of fabric, with God being the One with the knitting needles or weaving machine. A knitter takes different threads and knits them together to make a beautiful piece of fabric. A quilter takes different pieces of fabric and sews them together to make a beautiful quilt. God takes us as individual threads or fabrics of unique color, style and texture, strengths and weaknesses, and makes a beautiful tapestry. He cuts away, removes frayed edges, bonds together, and adds contrast and blends, yielding His handiwork to behold. Love, prayer, and the Holy Spirit will bond the team together even more. Thank God for His mighty hand as He adds, takes away, or brings change.

The goal for any ministry team should be to become a highly effective ministering team, accomplishing the team's mission and vision of the church or ministry. Below are team-building activities that I have found to be successful.

Team-Building Exercises

- Relationships are made stronger through the cohesion of fellowship. As individuals commune they can enjoy food and conversation. People tend to loosen up and become more personal during those times. Choose two to three times out of a year for the team to go out to a restaurant for breakfast, lunch, or dinner. Select a time that works well for the majority of your team. A team may choose to go to a restaurant after an event if the hour is not too late. Fellowshipping at the home of one of the team members can accomplish the same results. I recommend that at home fellowships each member bring a covered dish or dessert to share with everyone.

- Keep a calendar to celebrate the birthdays of team members. Our dance team recognizes and celebrates the birthdays within a given month. We have one person on the team who enjoys baking birthday cakes as a ministry gift. The birthday celebrations are incorporated in a team meeting.

- Replace a regular meeting or rehearsal session with team ministry. Minister to each other with words of exhortation and in the dance. Pray together as a team. Pray for each other. These ministry times are meant to comfort, exhort, and encourage. Refer to the Prophecy and Prophetic Dance chapter for more details.

- Work on a project together, such as making praise enhancers.

- Attend a dance workshop or conference together. This is time to build relationships, knowledge, and skill.

- Take a group picture. Make frames from card stock or foam and have each member sign his name or initials on each frame. Give each team member a copy of the team photo in the special signature team frame. The process will need to be repeated as new members join the team. I recommend that the new members be given plenty of time to adjust before taking a new group picture.

- Start a scrapbook for the team. Have someone take pictures of the team when the team ministers in dance. Have a scrapbook session and invite team members to write captions for each photo, or cut and paste pictures.

Partnering with the Worship Team

Once the pastor agrees that the dance team can function as a dance team during the weekly praise and worship service, the dance leader should then meet with the worship team leader to discuss how the two ministries can work together in unity during the worship services. The two leaders can share the vision and mission of each ministry as well as discuss how the teams together can help usher the people into the presence of God. The dance team can add to the worship service by dancing in the aisles. It is important that the dance team become familiar with the songs being sung by the worship team. Familiarity with the words and tempo of the music makes the development of movements easier.

The dance team can choreograph simple movements to accompany some of the praise and worship songs that are sung by the praise and worship team. This will help the team flow in unity. Simple choreographed movements will also help the team flow more uniformly. Refer to the chapter on choreography for more dance movement details. The dance team and worship team play a major part in leading the church into God's throne room. This partnership is vital.

Music, songs, dance, and prayer are all weapons of warfare that can be used mightily against the kingdom of darkness. Our sacrifice of prayer, praise, and worship goes before the Lord as a sweet smelling fragrance. Individually they can create a beautiful aroma that reaches the nostrils of God. Just imagine for a moment what takes place in the spirit realm whenever prayer, praise, worship, and dance are incorporated as an offering to God. God is moved to minister back to us!

> May my prayer be set before you like incense; may the lifting up of my hands be like the evening sacrifice.
> — Psalm 141:2

2: Temple Maintenance

The dance team is formed, all of the preliminaries are in place, and everyone on the team is eager to get started on the first dance. Before jumping right into the choreography of the first dance, some form of stretching exercises should be done. The level of flexibility for each individual will vary according to age and or experience.

We all have different body structures, shapes, and sizes. Certain body structures will naturally have more flexibility than others. When new people are introduced to the ministry of dance, they should be warned at the beginning not to overwork their muscles. Movements should be done in moderation, with a gradual increase of movements over time. Proper stretching should be done frequently to avoid injury. Stretching helps to condition the muscles and helps to reduce muscle soreness. Conditioning our bodies on a regular basis becomes even more important as we age.

There will probably always be some soreness in different muscle groups or body parts throughout our active participation in dance. We offer our body to the Lord as instruments of righteousness when we minister unto Him in the dance and by living according to the Word (Rom. 6:13). Since our bodies are the temple of the Holy Ghost, we are to care for our bodies as unto the glory of God! The priest of old spent quality time caring for the temple. In retrospect, we as priest of the new temple, which is our body, should become more diligent about temple maintenance. A healthy body can be gained and maintained through the development of healthy habits such as exercising, stretching, eating a balanced diet, and drinking plenty of water. Listed next are spiritual parallels to some of the physical activity needed for maintaining a healthy temple.

EXERCISING the physical body improves fitness, and builds endurance and stamina. Exercise your faith through hearing the word of God. Romans 10:17 tells us, "So then faith comes by hearing, and hearing by the word of God."

STRETCHING is extending in length our body parts. Improves flexibility and protects you from muscle strain, pulls, and soreness. Stretch and extend your faith; believe God to perform His Word and promises within your life.

WATER is an essential part of one's daily diet, and helps to cleanse the body of waste. Drink plenty of spiritual water, the Spirit of God, the Word of God, which cleanses us from all unrighteousness. Pray in the spirit, which is praying in tongues, allowing the rivers of living water to build up your spirit man.[1]

EAT a balanced diet. Feed your body the proper foods. Feed your spirit with the Word of God.

VITAMINS are used to supplement your diet. Balanced meals are important, but sometimes we eat on the go. Make it a good practice to supplement with vitamins. When you can't read the Word, listen to the Word on tape, listen to the Word on TV, or listen to the Word on the radio. Prayer is one of your spiritual vitamins. "Pray without ceasing."[2] Praise and worship are spiritual vitamins. They are spiritual nutrients that bring balance to your spiritual diet. Psalm 34:1 states, "I will bless the LORD at all times: his praise shall continually be in my mouth."

IT IS GOOD to practice good posture, which will help in the presentation of the dance. Posture yourself mentally to have a good attitude. Posture yourself spiritually to walk in love. Posture yourself to read the word so that your heart is changed. 1 Peter 3:15 states, "But sanctify the Lord God in your hearts: and be ready always to give an answer to every man that asks you a reason of the hope that is in you with meekness and fear."

GROOMING – Prepare your body. Prepare your spirit. Even though the outer appearance is important, God looks at the heart. We want our inner beauty to outweigh our outer beauty.

Muscle Strengthening

Good temple maintenance is important for physical endurance during a dance routine. The stretching of muscles will help prevent muscle strain and soreness. Muscle strengthening and conditioning builds strong muscles, allowing them to do their fair share of the work. Proverbs 31:17 talks about the virtuous woman, who girded her loins with strength and made her arms strong. She strengthened herself both spiritually and physically. We should follow her example in the sense of temple maintenance. We must strengthen our spirits by the Word of God and strengthen our physical bodies through muscle toning, conditioning, and stretching.

I have experienced chronic muscle and body aches because certain muscles were not functioning to their full potential. This caused other muscles to become over worked and stressed to the point of severe pain. As a result, the muscles became cramped and inactive due to lack of movement. Muscle spasms and trigger points developed in different areas of my body, which caused nagging aches, muscle tightness, and soreness. Prayer, therapy, reconditioning, and strengthening of the muscles helped to combat the muscle battle, working towards the goal of eventually eliminating the pain and soreness.

Keeping balance is important in everything that we do. Avoid over stressing or over stretching certain muscle groups.

A Note of Wisdom

Since our body is used as a weapon to war against the enemy, we should always plead the blood of Jesus over our body. Pray for God's divine protection; pray against injury, muscle strains, and pulls. As we praise God with our body, we wreak havoc in the enemy's camp. Therefore, our body becomes a major target for the enemy to attack. Thank God for the blood of Jesus and His mighty hedge of protection!

Helpful Hint

Aerobic exercise increases the heart rate and metabolism.

It will help with endurance during dance.

3: Choreography

Choreography begins by pulling together the dance technique, presentation style, and purpose. First starting with the song, we determine the message that is to be conveyed to the audience. Then the presentation style and dance technique should be considered.

When choreographing and coordinating a dance, we must remember that all dances are made up of a beginning, a body, and an end. Transitions are made from one movement to the next. Worship dances usually include slow, soft, smooth transitions as one moves from one position to the next position. Graceful turns and defined arm movements work well for worship. Praise dances can be more random and irregular, which would include faster moves and transitions such as a fast walk, skips, spins, or leaps.

There are many things to consider while choosing music or even movements for a dance in ministering. One, we must be prayerful to ask God which songs would be appropriate for the service. It is helpful to play a song, listen to the words, and just begin to move freely to see what movements will come for the dance. It is important not to become discouraged when the mental images of the movements do not come in chronological order, which allows us to link them together from the start to finish. As we play the song over and over, more movements will come. Develop good practice by listening to songs while freely dancing to them at home.

As a leader, we don't have to have it together all of the time. It's okay not to have a dance fully choreographed before teaching it to others. Remember this is a ministry and God requires that we walk by faith and trust Him. God wants our confidence to be in Him, knowing that He will provide by showing us the movements. Oftentimes God will wait to give some of the movements at the dance rehearsal session. Knowing that we don't have it all together when we go before the team requires a lot of faith. It is a requirement to prepare ourselves beforehand, but we should remain flexible for changes. If God doesn't give any of the dance movements before a rehearsal session, then we must trust that He will finish it or begin it at the rehearsal session. If the movements do not eventually begin to come, it's possible that God may be telling us to consider another song. Seeking the Lord for the right movements for the choreography will require sacrificing our time to go before Him. We must seek Him for the message that He desires to speak.

While the choreography of a dance is important, the positioning, placement and movements of each dancer will have a great impact on the presentation. The dance visually communicates to the congregation or audience. Dance tells a story, paints a picture, and speaks to the people through the choreography and presentation.

Choreography Tips to Use in Preparing Your Dance

- Pray before practice

- To avoid looking rushed in the dance, try to convey the general message of the lyrics without choreographing movements for every word of a song.

- Incorporate sign language whenever possible in interpretive dances. I have found that sign language is a great enhancement to dance movements, and also helps the dance to flow.

- Stay in sync with the melody of the song while dancing. This is done by ear, which will take practice. For example, if a choir is singing out of sync with the music, then the singing will sound off key. Likewise, if the movements are not flowing with the music, the dance will appear to be out of sync.

- Our facial expressions are an important element of the dance. Express on your face the emotion meant from the lyrics and tone of the song. Express the heart of God. Draw from the emotions of your soul to help convey the message.

- Whenever you want to emphasize a point, it is good to hold a dance position longer. Sometimes over exaggerating dance movements help emphasize points.

- Take advantage of the floor space available, by using it rather than dancing in a small area.

- When dancing in a group, spread the dancers out to avoid looking cluttered.

- Use movements at different levels to make the dance look more interesting. Some movements can be high in the air, some at floor level, and others in between.

- Add dynamics to the dance by having different dancers do different movements at different times. Transition from one group to another or one individual to another. This will prevent the dance from looking boring.

- Choose the right garment for the dance. It is good to have general costumes or garments that will complement many dances. Some dances will require specific garments to help convey the message.

- While singing is a part of worship, it shouldn't be done while dancing because it can be a distraction.

- Another big distraction is gum chewing while dancing.

- If using taped music to minister, use a high quality cassette tape to copy a song for dance. Poor quality recording is distracting. It is best to use the original CD or cassette whenever possible.

- Try using the mirroring technique during an entire dance or portions of a dance. Mirroring is when one person leads the group in dancing different movements. You can also rotate the leading person during these expressive praise moments.

- Incorporate props in choreography as another layer of praise.

Helpful Hint

Incorporate dramatic expressions within your choreography on some dances, which helps to stir imagination and emotions. This works well with interpretive and expressive worship type dances.

4: Props For Praise

We can incorporate props for praise by using various jewel toned colors in our choreography. The Temple of Solomon was uniquely designed with stones of various colors. The heavenly city is garnished with all manners of precious stones (Rev. 21:19). We can show forth the Lord's glorious splendor and majesty through the use of colors and props.

The heavens rejoice with us when we layer our praise with splendid colors that represent the Kingdom of God.

As mentioned earlier, King David was a creative worshiper. David not only sang, he danced, created music, wrote songs and poetry. He also created his own instruments of praise to worship the Lord.[1] He was not limited in expressing his gratitude and love to his Creator. As worshipers, we can be just as creative and make our own instruments for praise and worship.

Many time the scriptures referred to the ladies dancing with tambourines, but we are no longer limited to just the timbrel for dance. We can now make many types of instruments or props to worship the Lord in dance, such as streamers, praise hoops, praise cloths, banners, flags, and more.

I personally like to call props "praise enhancers" for the reason that props are added to the choreography as another layer of worship and used to enhance the message being communicated. A picture is worth a thousand words, and the human mind understands better when pictures are illustrated. If a portion of a dance can be illustrated in a more effective way with a streamer or flag, then by all means use them. If a song speaks of God's glory, then gold flag banners would fit perfectly into the choreography.

The art of dance itself transcends verbal communication and introduces visual communication. The words of a song are brought to life through the visual movements in a dance. Incorporating praise enhancers into a dance, together with a song will promote emphasis on a particular word or theme in the song. For

example, if a song speaks of rivers of praise, you may want to use a rhythmic streamer to emphasize the flow of water, or fabrics showing the colors of the sea. One might choose to run with the fabric to give the affect of flowing waters, or two people together might billow the fabric or ruffle the fabric to create water like waves. These billowing fabrics are called praise cloths. Praise cloths are excellent enhancers for worship. Explained on the next few pages are examples of different props that dancers use to enhance their expressions of worship. Allow God to expand your creativity through the making of your own instruments for praise.

Praise Enhancers

Praise Cloths

A praise cloth is approximately 4-5 yards of lightweight fabric. Lamé, lining, or organza fabrics are ideal for praise cloths. Finish off the ends of the fabric before use to avoid fraying the material.

During worship a dancer stands at each end of the praise cloth. While holding the edges of the fabric, the praise cloth is lifted high into the air. Then the cloth is allowed to slowly cascade down. This action is called billowing and can be repeated throughout the song. The dancers may choose to add more drama to the raising of the praise cloth by meeting each other in the center while the praise cloth is still in the air, or they can switch places while the cloth remains in the air. Swinging the cloth back and forth also makes a really nice effect. Ruffling the fabric will give a water wave effect. The air that is captured beneath the cloth is what yields such a nice billow form.

An individual dancer can use a praise cloth, but it would require cutting the fabric to a more manageable length. Try draping the cloth around the back of the neck, allowing the ends to cascade over the shoulders. Then run your fingers down to the ends of each side of the cloth and hold the corners of the cloth. Swing the arms from side to side, then step forward and swing both arms upward. Repeat the movements and have fun interjecting your own style.

Rhythmic Streamers

A rhythmic streamer is usually a long satin-like ribbon. Ribbons can be substituted with lamé fabric cut into ribbon length strips. Finish off the ends before use. The ribbon can be cut to any length that is manageable for dance. The ribbon portion is first attached to a swivel that allows flexibility and movement, and then attached to a stick like base. You can make your own base or purchase one (see Resources on the compact disc accompanying this book).

When dancing with ribbons, it is important to use large movements to prevent tangling. You can make large circles in front of you or over your head. Your grip on the base of the handle, whether it is palms down, or palms up will create different effects with the ribbon. Try to pivot around on the ball of the feet while making spiraling movements with the ribbon. Use the entire movement of your arm while turning the ribbon in small quick circles or hold arms stationary while flexing the wrist in different directions. The trick to this movement is the movement of the wrist. Moving the wrist in a circular motion helps to form small circles. You can flick the ribbon over your head and back or wave the ribbon from side to side. You can also make the ribbon look like water waves if you run with it and flick it, moving your hand up and down. Make large z-formations while turning in a circle. The z-formation in this case will be a z on its side to form the waves.

Praise Hoops

There are many variations of praise hoops. The hoops are available in different sizes, ranging from four inches to about eight inches in diameter. The hoop fringe is usually made of layered metallic strips or layered ribbon strips. The fringe usually covers about seven-eighths of the outer diameter of the hoop. A space on the outer edge is left opened for holding the hoop. The fringe can be cut to a desirable length. Some hoops are constructed as a timbrel with a fabric like material inserted halfway to slightly cover the inner circle of the hoop.

If there are enough hoops for everyone, it is always more artful when using two praise hoops at a time. Place one in each hand. Make circular motions with the hoops in front of you or slightly to your sides. Stretch your arms outward over your hips while turning with the hoops flowing in the air. The fringe looks beautiful in motion. You can make a similar movement with your arms stretched over your head. Praise hoops look great during presentation when the same movements are done by an entire group. Be creative and try new movements with the hoops. Praise hoops are just that, they are hoops made for praise. You are cheering for Jesus through movements with radiant colors that declare His majesty.

Flags and Flag Banners

Regular styled flags are designed with about three quarters of the flag covering the pole. The exposed portion of the flag pole gives easy access for carrying the flag. Some flags are made specifically to cover baton like flag poles. Flag banners are larger than the average size flags and cover the entire pole or dowel. The flag banners are usually lightweight, making it less tiring to hold. Jeweled tone lamé fabrics are suitable for the banner styled flags. Lamé and liquid styled fabrics work well for the large processional flags.

Flag banners can be used as a single flag or in pairs. The presentation of the flag banners looks great when used in pairs. The following movements are basic and can be applied to the use of one or more flags at a time. Take a flag in your hand, gripping it from either the end or center. The grip location will depend upon the type flag you are using. Wave the flag from side to side. Circle the flag while flexing the wrist, alternating directions to avoid tangling the flag. Move flag in a figure eight pattern. Hold the pole horizontally and flick or shake the flag to create a rippling effect. Try turning around in a circle with the flags adjacent to your underarms. This movement will make the flags appear to be wings under your arms. Using two flags of different colors in one hand gives a beautiful dual colored appearance.

WORD Banners

Word banners carry a message or words that exhort God. They are usually created under inspiration. Designs will vary depending upon the designer of the banner. These banners are majestic in presentation and display. They are used as a focal point during processionals or in specific parts of the choreography. Word banners are usually massive in size and are best carried on banner poles by men. The banner designs are magnificent in details of various fabrics, colors, jewels, fringes, and tassels along with words or symbols lining the banner body. These Word banners are usually embroidered with scriptures, names of God, or symbolic representation of those words.

Other Enhancers

Other props that could be useful in presentations are: crowns, pillows, mask, balls, candles, mirrors, scarves, hats, or anything that fits the message that you desire to convey.

Helpful Hint

The Rivers of Praise Worship Through Movement

Accompanying CD contains demonstrations

using praise enhancers.

Incorporate props in portions of the dance choreography to

emphasize, to enhance, or to increase the intensity of your ending.

5: Priestly Garments To Fit You For The King

The garments we select for the ministry of dance are just as significant as the dance presentation itself. The choice of garments is usually dependant upon one or two things, the presentation dance style, and the message that is to be conveyed through the dance.

Elegant flowing dresses, fitted bodices, and contoured sleeves are more befitting for dances that are heavily choreographed with ballet steps. The hip hop and African styled dances require garments suitable for the culture being portrayed. Expressive worship and interpretive dance are the least restrictive in garment selection since a combination of dance styles can be choreographed into one dance. As far as the ministry of dance goes, we must always be sensitive in choosing our dance garments. Modesty should come first in ministry. We could have a flawless presentation in our dance but miss the opportunity to get God's message through to our audience because they became so distracted by our lack of modesty in dress. Modesty in the dance ministry entails choosing movements and attire that are appropriate for presentation. Covering a tight bodice with an overlay is an example of modesty and may be necessary on some occasions. Wearing culottes under flowing skirts is another example of modesty in dress. Our primary goal in the dance is to minister unto the Lord, the King of kings. His Spirit then ministers to the hearts of the people through our dance presentation.

Queen Esther put on her royal apparel and stood in the inner court of the King's house. As the king sat on his throne, he noticed Esther and was pleased with her. He showed her favor as he held out his golden scepter, the rod of authority. Queen Esther did not choose just any garment to wear to approach the king, she chose her royal garments. She wanted to present herself well.

As we enter before our King Jesus to present our gift of praise to Him, we want to present ourselves with a look of royalty. Our beauty will enthrall our Lord.

> The king is enthralled by your beauty; honor him, for he is your lord. The Daughter of Tyre will come with a gift; men of wealth will seek your favor. All glorious is the princess within; her gown is interwoven with gold. In embroidered garments she is led to the king; her virgin companions follow her and are brought to you. They are led in with joy and gladness; they enter the palace of the king. — Psalms 45:11-15

The garments of the high priest were specially designed, dedicated, and consecrated for God's use. The priest wore these garments as he went before God offering gifts and making sacrifices unto Him. We are priests under the law of Grace. As ministers in dance, we should set aside garments to use specifically in ministering to the Lord, for offering our sacrifices of praise. We are to clothe ourselves with righteousness as we clothe our bodies with garments made for praise.

When God gave the blue print for the design and building of the Tabernacle, He also gave a blue print for the design of the garments that were to be worn only by the priest. Exodus chapters 28 and 29 give the instructions and designs for both the Tabernacle and priestly garments. These sacred garments were made for Aaron and his sons to serve as priest. King David also wore a linen robe layered with an ephod and sash. David was a king, but he dressed in priestly attire whenever he ministered unto God, bringing burnt offerings and peace offerings before the Holy One. Our garments don't necessarily have to be linen because we now have a variety of different textured fabrics, tapestries, and fiber mixes. This is by no means a comprehensive listing because the fabric mix is constantly changing. The chart also provides examples and ideas for the design of your personal or team dance garments.

Type of Fabric	Garments
Bridal Satin	Vest, Ephod, Overlay
Brocade	Vest, Ephod
Charmeuse	Dress, Skirts
Chiffon	Overlays for tops or skirts
Cotton	Skirts, Dress, Leotard, Practice Pants
Cotton Interlock	Practice Pants and Shirts
Crepe de Chine	Circle Skirts, Pants
French Terry	Practice Pants and Shirts
Georgette	Circle Skirts
Jersey	Practice Pants and Shirts
Lamé	Vest, Ephod, Overlay or Culottes
Lamé Quilted	Vest, Ephod
Linen	Vest, Ephod, Overlay
Lining	Culottes, Vest
Lycra	Skirts, Dress, Leotard
Moiré Taffeta	Vest, Ephod, Overlay
Panne Velvet	Skirts, Dress, Leotard
Sequin	Vest, Tops, Belts, wrist or head bands
Silk Essence	Dress, Skirts, Pants, Vest
Spandex Knit	Skirts, Dress, Leotard, Practice Pants
Taffeta	Vest, Ephod, Overlay
Velvet	Dress, Vests, Leotards, Pants, Skirts
Washable Silks	Dress, Skirts, Pants, Vest, Culottes

Jewels, beads, sequins, and metallic trims can be used to enhance or beautify the garments to give a royal look.

To properly construct a garment there are important measurements to consider, some of which are listed in the Measurement Guide (see included CD).

Significance of Color

The colors of our dance garments can play a significant part in helping to interpret the message being communicated. God uses colors in various scriptures to communicate His truth to us. In the scriptures, colors were very symbolic. The following chart details colors, their meanings, and scripture references.[1]

Table of Symbolic Colors

Color	Message	Scriptures
Amber	The glory of God	Ezek. 1:4, 8:2
Black	Sin, death, famine	Jer. 8:21, 14:1-2; Lam. 4:4-8; Rev. 6:5
Blue	Heavenly, authority from above, Holy Spirit, healing	Exod. 24:10; Num. 4:7,9, 15:38; Prov. 20: 30; Ezek. 1:26, 10:1, 23:6; John 14:26
Crimson	Blood atonement, sacrifice or death	Lev. 14:52; Josh. 2:18, 21; Isa. 1:18
Gray	Dignity, honor, age	Gen. 42:38, Deut. 32:25; 1 Sam 12:2; Job 15:10; Ps. 78:18; Prov. 16:31; Hos. 7:9
Green	Prosperity, growth, life	Gen. 1:30; Exod. 10:15; Job 8:16; Ps. 23:2; Song of Sol. 2:13; Mark 6:39; Luke 23:31
Purple	Kingship, royalty	Judg. 8:26; John 19:2
Red	War, bloodshed, death	2 Kings 3:22; Rev. 6:4; 12:3
Scarlet	Blood atonement; sacrifice (as crimson)	Lev 14:52; Joshua 2:18, 21; Isa 1:18
White	Purity, light, righteousness, holiness of God, Christ, angels or saints	Rev. 3:4-5, 6:2, 7:9, 15:6, 19:8

Choosing the appropriate garment for each dance is a skill in itself. If you desire to covey a message using a particular color and you don't have the garments to match, you can use a piece of fabric that color.

We tend to build our daily wardrobes with basic colors and styles. We can do the same with our dance garments, starting with the basics and build from there. A basic dance wardrobe could start with a white dress or a white skirt and top, a white leotard and tights with white or pink ballet shoes, while choosing colorful vests or overlays for variety.

If you choose not to start with white, then the royal or jewel toned colors could be chosen as the main garments with white leotards, tights, and white or pink ballet shoes. Black ballet or jazz shoes are also available and can be used as basic starters. Different teams will have different styles and preferences; therefore, we must be prayerful, and choose what is best for the team.

The style of a garment choice depends on the type of dance used to minister. If we're doing a dance with a lot of rolling on the floor or stepping, then we should wear a loose pant design instead of a skirt to prevent exposing undergarments. Culottes or leggings should be worn under any of the dress and skirt garments for the same reason. Layering the clothing when light colored fabrics are worn is also recommended in order to maintain modesty. We should minimize the amount of jewelry that is worn during ministry. Too much jewelry can become a distraction to the audience and a weighty obstacle for the dancer. We are the messengers. How we are "packaged" will make a difference in how the people receive the message. We must stay focused on the fact that people can easily become distracted.

Common Distractions

- See through clothing — you want people to see the movements being emphasized and not your undergarments
- Torn garments
- Spotted or dingy garments, especially white garments
- Runs in tights
- Bouncing breast
- Colorful bras under white garments or leotards (use basic black or white)
- Tassels hanging out of ballet shoes
- Big jewelry
- Exposed unshaven under arms
- Circle or flare skirts without culottes

Helpful Hints

Purchase sports bras especially for dance. Purchase culottes, lined skirts, and ballet or jazz shoes for dance. Modest attire is an absolute requirement to minister before God and His people. Our ministry can enhance the worship service or it can become a distraction!

Establish early responsible parties for garments and uniforms owned by the church. An example of a uniform agreement is included on the CD accompanying this book. Follow the provided garment care guide to help extend the life of your garments.

6: Empowering Youth To Worship God

Our knowledge and understanding of how we can worship through movement has expanded. This very same knowledge can be passed on to the next generation. We can become better mentors to the youth in our lives by sharing and enlightening their hearts about worship. We can encourage them now to catch the eternal wave of worship!

As we challenge the young people, both boys and girls, to worship God with all of their gifts and talents, we help them escape the traditional thinking about worship and praise. Traditional thinking says that you praise God only in church while singing a song. Traditional thinking also says that you only praise God while in a church setting. Many people are not aware of the true meaning of worship. In most cases, people feel that worship is just saying, "Thank you Jesus." In worshipping God, one speaks of God's character, speaks of His mighty ways, speaks of His awesome love, and speaks of His great mercy and extreme grace. The youth must learn to magnify God with worship whether it is in prayer, in song, in dance, in a poem, in painting, in music, or in their life style. Teach the youth that worship is all about God! Praise is unto God for what He has done, for what He is doing, and for what He has promised to do. As the true meaning of praise and worship and understanding is developed, they will become effective ministers. We can teach them about the attitudes of the heart since attitudes are a critical factor in being a faithful minister. The youth must understand that in everything they do they must give God glory. Teaching them about what the Word says about praise and about our heart as worshipers will help keep their motives pure and their focus in the right perspective.

Young people enjoy music and songs, they enjoy games, and

they enjoy sports. Young people enjoy having fun. A leader in the arts ministry must be creative, making the ministry appealing to the youth in order to attract them. If you are working with a youth dance team, build in a variety of different style dances for worship that are fun and lighthearted. Since the youth usually enjoy songs that are upbeat, selecting contemporary Christian music is probably a good choice. When choreographing a praise dance for the youth, you could incorporate modern, hip hop, or jazz style movements that are playful, lively, and filled with attitude. Most teens or youth will enjoy "kicking it" for Christ! Help the youth BREAKTHOUGH the kingdom of darkness with PRAISE, while they learn to minister unto the Lord with worshipful songs. They will learn to be more graceful in their dance movements when dancing to a song of worship.

Managing a Team with a Variety of Ages

While serving as the director of the arts ministry at a previous church, a variety of ages diversified our dance team. To help manage the different age groups, we divided the dance ministry into three teams. The children's team ranged from ages five to eleven, the teenage group ranged from ages twelve to seventeen, and the adult team included anyone eighteen and over. As the leader over the arts ministry, I had the responsibility of teaching or delegating others to teach the different teams.

Dance rehearsals for each age group were scheduled at different times. Special care was taken with the children's group to avoid distractions. Parents were asked to drop off their little ones and return after the rehearsal. Basic ballet movements and sign language were incorporated into the children's dances. One or two adults or teens were selected to learn the children's dances so that they might dance along with the children and help them remember each movement. The choreography for the teen and adult teams had more technical movements, complex steps, and transitions.

Each dance team was assigned one Sunday out of each month to minister with a dance presentation. The mime and drill team also ministered during each month. On special occasions, we would choreograph a dance to include all of the dancers. Many times the dances would compliment the message in the pastor's sermon. It was always nice to see how God would bring the entire church service together. The choir sang about the Word, the pastor spoke the Word, and the ministering arts through dance, mime, or drill teams, demonstrated the Word.

Steps to Take to Challenge the Youth

- Teach the youth how to pray. Tell them that prayer is more than just Psalm 23 or the 'The Lord's Prayer.' Teach them to pray scripture. Let them start with a simple verse like Philippians 4:13, *"I can do all things through Christ which strengthens me"* and tell them to add other scriptures to their prayer. Daily prayer is essential to building a healthy relationship with Jesus Christ.

- Ask them what their interests are such as, music, singing, dancing, acting, drawing, writing, speaking, sports, computer games, band, etc. Have them write them down, and submit them to you. The leader should review each list.

- Ask each youth to identify each area of interest in which they are already involved and to what degree.

- Encourage the youth by telling them that wherever they are already committing their time can become praise to God, if they keep positive attitudes while doing that activity. Teach them to give thanks to God for their gifts and talents. Tell them to ask God for His help to do the activity in a more excellent way. Remind them to give God thanks at all times for helping them and for being with them. (You are now at a good stage to help them advance in praise.)

- Challenge them to become more than spectators during praise and worship services at church. Challenge them to become participants by taking an active part in the worship service. They can praise along with the choir or praise leaders. Suggest that they join the dance, mime, drama, or drill ministry teams where applicable.

- Tell them that "praise looks good on them" and that they are building their personal relationship with God through their praise. God enjoys them individually. God is pleased with their praise.

- Teach them to pray, putting on the whole armor of God for divine protection. As they step out in the area of praise,  the enemy will try to bring discouragement. Remind them that the Word of God is their greatest weapon, followed by prayer and praise. They are to allow God to fight the battles by His Spirit.

- Teach the youth about the "Character of Christ" and "Relationship with Christ" to help build their spiritual foundation.

Helpful Hint

Teach the youth to ask the question, "What would Jesus do?"

before they make a decision.

Let the young people know that praising God is a cool thing to

do. Take them through the exercise of acting out different forms of

worship as stated in the "Praise Unlimited Mall."

7: Looking Ahead
The Ministering Arts in Evangelism

If my people, who are called by my name, will humble themselves and pray and seek my face and turn from their wicked ways, then will I hear from heaven and will forgive their sin and will heal their land. — 2 Chronicles 7:14

Who is this scripture referring to? We, the believers of Jesus Christ are called by His name. As followers of Christ the Aointed One, we are called Christians. Revelation 5:5 refers to Jesus as the Lion of Judah, and as stated in the "Pattern of Worship" chapter, Judah is the priesthood in the New Covenant.

As the scripture states, we are to humble ourselves, pray, seek His face, and turn from our ways that are not Christ-like. To seek His face is to seek His presence. We are to desire His presence and to search Him out. We are to seek out His insight. We need to know His perception and His view of things. We need to know His vision, purpose, and truth. Once we see the truth concerning our hearts we will be moved to turn from those wicked ways that hinder our growth in God; then God will hear from heaven and move on our behalf. Our prayers that ascend into the heavens will be heard and God will heal our land. God will not only heal our way, but He will heal our country, the nations, and the world.

The church is at a pivotal point where God is beckoning His bride to draw near to Him to seek His presence like never before, and seek to understand His truth. We have been in a place of seeking His provision, but we must add to that and seek His vision about everything concerning our lives. God will show us the truth about our hearts, and this will cause us to turn from those ways that are not like Him and be healed. As this is done corporately as the body of Christ, we will see our entire nation and world healed and changed. The Spirit of God will be evangelizing the world. John 12:32 speaks of the ascension of Jesus, but if Jesus is lifted up in our hearts (in this earth) then He will draw all men unto Himself. If His character and His ways are exemplified in our life then He will draw all people unto Himself. It's a promise.

Just think; every person that was healed by Jesus wanted to run and tell somebody else what happened. They wanted to give God praise. So, what is going to break open the dam that hinders praise? It is truth and once truth is revealed, we began to adapt, change, and we become healed; then a whole new level of resounding praise begins to flow out of our hearts, springing forth in the nations.

God desires that the entire world be evangelized with the Word of truth, the Gospel of Good News. The performing arts will be used as a catalyst of evangelism in the end-time revivals and outreaches. Praise will attract the people so that they may hear the Gospel.

I believe God will use the ministering arts as a key element to bring in a great harvest. In order to be used in this magnitude, we must be totally free in our praise. We must walk in obedience to God. We must trust God to minister in new fresh ways. We cannot be bound by fear. We cannot be bound by the traditions of man, nor can we box God into a set of familiar patterns. God has a way, but we must trust Him to show us the way.

God desires to reach a harvest of people who are not bound by tradition. This harvest of people who have not yet learned the ways and traditions of the church, are in the highways and by-ways. God is raising up a new breed of worshipers who, at all cost, will follow the leading of the Holy Spirit. They will execute judgment against the enemy through their praise, reclaiming souls for the Kingdom of God. In order to reach this "un-traditionalized" people, we must go where they are, which is outside of the church walls. God is raising up worship teams and dance teams within the church, first to minister to Him, then to free the people in the pews to praise God with more liberty. A large portion of their commission will become outreach. I believe we will see ministering arts teams in the church for the purpose of evangelism. The ministering arts will begin to come out of the church walls and out of the woodwork, and overflow into the highways and by-ways for the advancement of the Kingdom. We will see arts in the street, arts in the park, and the arts after God's own heart.

The presentations, I foresee, will be regal, full of excellence and magnificence, suited to represent the King of kings and Lord of lords. The presentations will reflect the character of God, as well as His love and heartfelt desire for saving the lost. The splendid array of colors will be eye catching and draw the by-standers. The rhythm of the music and the sound of praise will entice the curious to come. The lyrics of the songs will speak to the hearts of the people. The dance movements, gestures, love, and passion for God will be expressed to solidify the message, while the Holy Spirit captures the hearts. The anointing of God will begin to break the yokes to heal and deliver the people. People will long to experience this type of relationship with Christ.

Some might say that this type of outreach would appear as entertainment because it is outside the church walls. After they witness, experience, or hear about the power of God manifesting in such manner, where hundreds of thousands are evangelized into the Kingdom, their opinions will change. They will know then that God has appropriated the arts to minister in this dimension and with great magnitude.

It is imperative that we walk by faith and believe God for great exploits. I foresee open field revivals, revivals without walls springing forth with the ministering arts being a catalyst for evangelism. The Word will go forth and the arts in movement will go forth. This will be a season of marching, crossing over barriers, and tearing down denominational walls. Praise and worship promotes unity, and one accord in one spirit. Certain traditions that have held us bound will be broken. This will be a season of breaking the norms and opposing the status quo of what the world perceives about the church, which will usher in a ground- breaking move of God. I even envision "praise parades," breaking forth in different cities where the musicians will play, the singers will sing, the praise dancers will dance, mime and dramatizations will be done on moving stages. Flags, streamers, and banners will leave colorful paths to draw the masses. These parades will go forth in a processional like fashion. The sound of praise will be heard afar. The preached word will be spoken over loud speakers to capture the hearts for Jesus. Witnessing tracks will be handed out to by-standers while the prayer warriors intercede for victory. Who knows what God might do in a wide-open setting like that? Why not miracles, signs and wonders? God will cause His righteousness and praise to spring forth in the earth.

During this coming season, God's people will be challenged to walk in a higher level of obedience to the Word. We will be held accountable to live a holy upright life in accordance with God's standards. We must be intensely sensitive to the Holy Spirit so that we may flow with God. This would be a perfect time for the intercessors to unite with the praise and worshipers in the fullness of the ministry, together believing God for increase for the Kingdom.

We are called ministers, anointed to preach the good news, to help bind up the broken hearted, to proclaim freedom to the captive, to release those that are in darkness, and to comfort those who mourn. God promised to give a crown of beauty in the place of ashes, the oil of gladness in the place of mourning, and a garment of praise in place of despair. We are in dark times, but God desires to shine in us and through us to encourage and draw the lost. God desires to display His Splendor through His Living Body!

Don't be afraid of this coming season. Just let go and let God. As we pray and intercede, the Spirit of God will prepare us and prepare the way.

> For as the soil makes the sprout come up and a garden causes seeds to grow, so the Sovereign LORD will make righteousness and praise spring up before all nations.
>
> — Isaiah 61:11

Notes Of Encouragement

A Note for All

Throughout this book we have discussed the heart of our being, the central focal point for character development, and what God expects of us as worshipers, dancers, and ministers unto the Lord.

Please remember that growing in the fruit of the Spirit is a process. Just as it takes time for the farmer to see fruit from the field he has planted, it will take time for us to see fruit from our spiritual planting. As you seek God for more in your spiritual walk with Him, He will begin to highlight areas in your life, usually a few at a time, on which you must begin to work. The next step is to search the scriptures concerning those areas in your life. As time passes and as you continue to bring those challenging areas to God and His promises to you, you will begin to see changes. Fruit of the Spirit will grow, develop, and become more evident in your life. Your loved ones, who know you the best, will especially see the changes occurring in your life. We are all striving to be more like Jesus, so don't be too hard on yourself and by no means give up!

A Note for the Leader

Learn the vision of your church. Seek input from the pastor on how a dance ministry can help to bring the church's vision to pass. Once you have received a green light to go forth, develop a vision or mission statement for the dance ministry. Then submit a copy of the statement and share it with your pastor. Hebrews 13:17 speaks about being in submission to leadership. Develop guidelines for the dance ministry and work to get the dance ministry added as an auxiliary to the church.

Know that praisers are always on the front line, like in the battle of Jehosaphat, and that the enemy will target you and try to discourage you. Therefore, be on guard and stay prayed up. Stay encouraged. There will be times you will have to encourage yourself. Remember, if God is for you, then who can be against you.

Stand firm on the things that God has given you. Go forth with excitement in the Lord. God will provide you with the resources. Refer to this book and the other resources listed on the CD that accompanies this book. These materials are designed to encourage and support you in what you've been called to do.

My prayer is that God continue to bless you and the dance ministry team. In all that you do, do it as unto the Lord!

About the Author

Rachel L. Moore is an ordained and licensed minister, dancer, and instructor who has assisted churches in establishing dance and performance art ministries for over 14 years. She ministers in expressive worship, interpretive and prophetic dance.

Rachel's desire is to see the lives of people changed through biblical truths, and to help release people in their praise unto God. Rachel also designs worship garments, props, dancer accessories, and other tools which are available through www.riversofpraise.com and selected stores.

In addition to her worship ministry, Rachel is a process control engineer. She and her husband, Johnny, have three sons and reside in Lizella, Georgia. To schedule training with Rachel for your church or ministry, contact Dawn Treader Publications at the address listed in the front of this book or online at www.riversofpraise.com.

Notes

Unless otherwise indicated, Scripture quotations are from The Holy Bible, New International Version (NIV), The King James Version of the Bible (KJV), or New American Standard Bible® (NASB).

Rivers of Praise (What does it mean?)
1. *Merriam Webster's New Collegiate Dictionary*, 9th ed., s.v. "river"
2. Ps. 8:3-9
* Additional Scripture References: Ps. 46:4; Rev. 22:1,2

Spiritual Elements
The Pattern for Worship
1. Jer. 31:31-34
2. *Nelson's Illustrated Bible Dictionary*, s.v. "Kidron"
3. Heb. 10:22, 24
4. *Biblesoft's New Exhaustive Strong's Numbers and Concordance*, s.v. "OT:2114, zuwr"
5. Ibid., s.v. "OT:7000, Qatar"
* Additional Scripture References: Exod. 26:33; 1 Kings 8; 1 Chron. 15, 16; 2 Chron. 1, 5, 30:9; John 14:26, 19:34; Rom. 12:1,2; 1 Tim. 2:1-8; Heb. 4:16, 9:1-28, 10:19-22; 1 Pet. 2:4-5; 1 John 2:27, 4:9-10

The Word of God — Our Biblical Cord to Eternal Life
1. *Nelson's Illustrated Bible Dictionary*, s.v. "the Word"
2. Heb. 5:12-13
3. Pss. 77:12, 143:5
4. Ps. 119:15, 48
5. Ps. 39:3; 2 Cor. 4:6
6. Dr. Bill Hamon, *Prophets Pitfalls and Principles*, (Shippensburg: Destiny Image, 1991), p. 198
* Additional Scripture References: Gen. 1:26-28; Col. 1:15-23; John 1:13,14, 14:26

The Chambers of God – The Passageway of Faith
* Additional Scripture References: Luke 8:11-15; Rom. 10:17, 14:1; Heb. 11:1-34

Secret Hiding Place — Prayer as a Place of Refuge
1. The Dancer's Prayer is comprised of: Neh. 8:10; Pss. 26:2, 100:4, 139:23-24; Matt. 5:23-24; John 4:24
2. Key Elements to an Effective Prayer, additional scriptures: Pss. 51:10-12, 100:4; Matt. 5:23-24; 2 Cor. 1:20; Eph. 6:18; Col. 4:2; Heb. 12:28-29; 1 John 1:9
* Additional Scripture References: Prov. 3:5-6; Matt. 6:6, 7:7-8, 18:20; Luke 11:13, 18:1; Acts 2:3-4, 11; Rom. 8:26-28; 1 Cor. 12:4-11, 14:4; 2 Cor. 10:3-6; Eph. 3:20, 6:11-12, 18; Phil. 4:6-7; Col. 1:9-14; 1Thess. 5:16-18; Heb. 4:16; James 5:16-18; 1 John 5:14-15

Relationship with Christ
1. The Prayer for the Divine Connection with God is comprised of: John 3:16-17; Rom. 10:9-10
2. *Merriam Webster's New Collegiate Dictionary*, 9th ed., s.v. "umbilical cord"
3. Song of Sol. 5:16
* Additional Scripture References: Gen. 1:26-28; 1 Sam. 16:13; Neh. 12:36; Isa. 61:10-11

Cultivating the Heart
1. 1 Cor. 3:1-3; Rom. 8:6-9
2. I learned the definitions of the five-fold (ascension) gifts at a session featuring Drs. David and Vernette Rosier; Eph. 4:11-16
3. Prov. 20:27; Rom. 8:27; 1 Cor. 2:10-11
4. The Prayer for Our Heart is comprised of: Ps. 7:9; Prov. 3:5-6, 4:23, 20:27; Jer. 17:9-10; Luke 4:18-19; Rom. 8:27; 1 Cor. 2:10,11
5. Prov. 20:5
6. 2 Sam. 22:29
7. *Merriam Webster's New Collegiate Dictionary*, 9th ed., s.v. "judgment"
8. Ibid., s.v. "haughty"
9. Ibid., s.v. "disdain"
10. Ibid., s.v. "peevish"
11. Jer. 1:5
12. 1 Tim. 1:5
13. The Prayer to Cultivate Our Hearts is comprised of: Pss. 51:10; 19:14, James 3:17-18
* Additional Scripture References: Pss. 19:4, 26:2-3, 51:10-12, 86:11-13, 143:10; Prov. 15:4; Isa. 14: 12-14; Ezek. 28:5-19; Matt. 12:34, 22:37; Mark 12:30, Luke 10:27; John 15:8-10; Rom. 12:2; 2 Cor. 10:3-6; Gal. 5:18-21, 24-25; Eph. 4:11-14, 26-27, 6:10-12; Heb. 5:12-14; James 3:1-18, 4:6-7; 1 Pet. 3: 10-11, 5:8-9; 1 John 4:8, 16-18; Rev. 12:7-10
14. Juanita Bynum, *Matters of the Heart* (Lake Mary: Charisma House, 2002)

Submitting Our Will for God's Way
* Scripture References: Rom. 13:1; Heb. 12:9-11, 13:17; James 3:17-18; 1 Pet. 5:4-11

Praise Unlimited
1. Matt. 27:27; John 19:23
2. Exod. 28:33-35
3. *Biblesoft's New Exhaustive Strong's Numbers and Concordance*, s.v. "OT:8416, tehillah"
4. Ibid., s.v. "OT:8426, towdah"
5. Ibid., s.v. "OT:3034, yadah"
6. Ibid., s.v. "OT:1288, barak"
7. Ibid., s.v. "OT:2167, zamar"
8. *Nelson's Illustrated Bible Dictionary*, s.v. "musical instruments of the Bible"
9. *Biblesoft's New Exhaustive Strong's Numbers and Concordance.*, s.v. "OT:1984, halal"
10. Ibid., s.v. "OT:7623, shabach"
* Additional Scripture References: Heb. 13:15; Isa. 61:3, 61:11

Application Elements
The Word on Dance
1. Debbie Roberts, *Rejoice: A Biblical Study of the Dance* (Shippensburg: Revival Press, 1982), p. 29-30
2. Ibid., p. 1
3. David Swan, *The Power of Prophetic Worship* (Kuala Lumpur, Malaysia: Tabernacle of David, 2001), p. 85-86
4. Murray Silberling, *Dancing for Joy, a Biblical Approach to Praise and Worship* (Baltimore: Lederer Messianic Publishers, 1995), p. 54-55
5. Neh. 8:10
6. Roberts, op. cit. pp. 90-91
7. *Biblesoft's New Exhaustive Strong's Numbers and Concordance.*, s.v. "OT:7812, shachah"
8. Todd Farley, *The Silent Prophet* (Shippensburg: Destiny Image, 1989), pp. 71-72, 75
9. *Biblesoft's New Exhaustive Strong's Numbers and Concordance.*, s.v. "NT:1411, dunamis"
10. Mark 5:30

*   Additional Scripture References: Exod. 15:20; 1 Sam. 29:5; Pss. 22:3; 42:4; 68:24-26; 117:1-2; 150:1-6; Luke 6:23, 15:25-27; Acts 17:28

Ministry Mission
1.   Mark 6:20-26
2.   Exod. 15:20-21

Technical Methods for the Ministry of Dance
1.   Heb. 13:20-21
2.   Jeremiah 9:17-20
3.   Farley, op. cit. pp. 76-77
4.   *Technical Manual and Dictionary of Classical Ballet,* Third Revised Edition, New York: Dover Publications, 1982
5.   Silberling, op. cit. p. 23
6.   Ibid., p. 49
7.   Ibid., p. 27
8.   *TheFreeDictionary.com* (Huntingdom Valley: Farlex, Inc., 2003), s.v. "dance terminolgy"
9.   Ibid.
10.   Hamon, op. cit. p. 199
11.   Aimee Verduzco Kovacs, Ph.D., *Dancing into the Anointing, Touching the Heart of God through Dance* (Shippensburg: Treasure House, 1996), pp. 58-59
12.   Ibid., p. 47
13.   *The Healing Art of African Dance,* Wyoma, Boulder: Sounds True, Inc., 1997, videocassette

Spiritual Warfare and Winning Battles
1.   1 John 4:4; Isa. 54:17
2.   Rev. 12:7-13, 17
3.   Zech. 4:6; Eph. 6:12; 2 Cor. 10:3-5
4.   Eph. 6:13-20
5.   Kovacs, op. cit. p. 47
6.   Ann Stevenson, *Restoring the Dance* ((Shippensburg, PA: Treasure House, 1997), p. 120

Prophecy and Prophetic Dance
1.   *Vine's Expository Dictionary of Old and New Testament Words,* s.v. "prophecy"
2.   Kovacs, op. cit. pp. 59-60
3.   Eph. 4:11-12
4.   Hamon, p. 195
5.   Ibid.
6.   Farley, op. cit. p. 87
7.   Ibid., pp. 82-83
8.   Kevin J. Conner, *Interpreting the Symbols and Types* (Portland: Bible Temple Publishing, 1980), p. 46
9.   I heard this at a prophetic conference featuring Steve Thompson on August 23, 2001.
10.   Deborah K. Smith leads Vessels of Honor at Harvest Cathedral Church, Georgia.
11.   Exod. 15:20; Ps. 150:4

Practical Elements
Organizing a Dance Team
1.   *Merriam Webster's New Collegiate Dictionary,* 9th ed., s.v. "team"
2.   The stages of team development were extracted from a course I attended in October 1994, at the Daniel Management Center, College of Business Administration, University of South Carolina. The course material was based on the work of Bruce W. Tuckman, 1965, and Mark Kelly, *The Adventures of a Self-Managing Team.*

3. Creflo Dollar, *Exposing the Spirit of Competitive Jealousy* (College Park: World Changers Ministries, 1993), pp. 1-3

4. Ibid.

5. Katzenbach and Smith, "Team Types and Definitions," *The Wisdom of Teams*, 1993

Temple Maintenance

1. Jude 20

2. 1Thess. 5:17

Props for Praise

1. 2 Chron. 7:6, 29:26-29

Priestly Garments to Fit You for the King

1. Conner, loc. cit.

2. 2 Kings 1:3-12

Glossary

Anointing - Special endowment or power, gift of the Holy Spirit; "but as the same anointing teaches you concerning all things, and is true, and is not a lie" (1 John 2:27). Often symbolized by oil (ex. James 5:14, Exod. 3:11). The anointing destroys the yoke (Isa. 10:27)

Choreography - The composition and arrangement of dance movements; joining of specific coordinated movements and transitions. Choreography requires having the ability to see movement, to connect steps, and the ability to inclusively balance with flowing transitions.

Dance - A series of rhythmic and patterned bodily movements usually performed to music. In the sense of ministry dance, this would be ministry and not performance. Dancing developed as a natural expression of united feeling and action.

Ministry - A distinctive biblical idea that means to serve. In reality, all believers are "ministers." The apostle Paul urged the true pastor-teacher to "equip the saints" so they can minister to one another (Eph. 4:1-12). Our model is Jesus, who did not come to be served, but to serve (Mark 10: 45). As servants of the Lord we minister in dance unto God and He ministers to the people through our movements and expression.

Pageantry - A colorful and splendid display of the Arts in Worship with dancers carrying banners, flags, and pillows with crowns on them to worship the King.

Prophecy - "Signifies the speaking forth of the mind and counsel of God. It is the declaration of that which cannot be known by natural means. It is the forth-telling of the will of God, whether with reference to the past, the present, or the future." (*Vines*)

Praise - An act of worship or acknowledgment by which the virtues or deeds of another are recognized and extolled. We are to praise God both for who He is and for what He does (Ps. 150: 2). Praising God for who He is, is called adoration. Praising Him for what He does is known as thanksgiving.

Processionals - A group of individuals moving along in an orderly, often ceremonial way (ex. walking in a single file carrying flags or dancing in the isles).

Prophetic Presbytery - 1 Timothy 4:14; when two or more prophets or prophetic ministers lay hands on and prophesy over an individual or individuals for a specific purpose, such as setting aside to do a particular work in the ministry. The Prophetic Presbytery also ministers prophetic rhema words, and imparts and activates individuals to their God-appointed offices, gifts, and callings.

Religious Spirits - Demonic spirits that use religion to bind, manipulate, control, confuse, destroy, divide, and conquer. Individuals under the influence of these spirits use religion in defense of their sin.

Rhema - A word or illustration that God speaks directly to a person that addresses that person's particular circumstance. (See also Heb. 6:5 and Rom. 10:17)

Types and Symbols - "Spiritual truths, ideas, thoughts, may be represented by material symbols, whether actions, institutions, or objects. In Scripture, frequent instances occur of such symbolical methods of conveying ideas; as, for instance, the placing of the hand under the thigh for confirmation of an oath, were signs to the people. In Romans 5:14, Adam is said to be the type of Christ." (*McClintock and Strong Encyclopedia*)

Vessel - In respect to the Christian, vessel refers to people who carry within them the knowledge of God. They are carriers of the Spirit of God and should freely pour out their gifts in love to someone in need. (See 2 Cor. 4:6-7 and Rom.9:21-23).

Worship - Reverent devotion and allegiance pledged to God; the rituals or ceremonies by which this reverence is expressed. The English word *worship* comes from the Old English word *worthship*, a word that denotes the worthiness of the one receiving the special honor or devotion. In Old Testament times Abraham built altars to the Lord and called on His name (Gen. 12:8; 13:18). This worship of God required no elaborate priesthood or ritual. New Testament worship is characterized by joy and thanksgiving because of God's gracious redemption in Christ. This early Christian worship focused on God's saving work in Jesus Christ. True worship was that which occurred under the inspiration of God's Spirit (John 4:23-24; Phil. 3:3).

Additional copies of *Rivers of Praise Worship Through Movement* and other titles from Dawn Treader Publications are available at your local bookstore, online at www.riversofpraise.com, or directly from the Publisher.

Dawn Treader Publications
He who treads the dawn is the Bright and Shining Morning Star™

A ministry of Morning Star And Company, Inc.
PO Box 22175
Beachwood, OH 44122

www.dawntreaderpublications.com
www.morningstarandcompany.org

Colophon

Set in Goudy Old Style and Goudy Sans

Cover Art, Layout and Design by KAR at Studio Downstairs, Inc.
Special Thanks to Editor-in-Chief, Annie S. Thomas
Author Photograph by Royal Andrews
Dancer Photographs by Johnny Moore and KAR
Printed and Bound in the United States of America
Special Thanks to Cheryl Corey at McNaughton & Gunn, Inc.

This book includes an Interactive Compact Disc.

Autorun will automatically play this disc
or browse to CD and click autorun.exe.
It is recommended that screen resolution
be set to 1024x768. Updates and downloads
available at www.riversofpraise.com.

Additional compact discs may be obtained
from the Publisher or by visiting www.riversofpraise.com.